C000260933

Reflections on the Sunday Gospel
(Year A)

Reflections on the Sunday Gospel

(Year A)

How to More Fully Live Out
Your Relationship with God

+

POPE FRANCIS

Curated by
Pierluigi Banna and Isacco Pagani

HODDER &
STOUGHTON

First published in Great Britain in 2022 by Hodder & Stoughton
An Hachette UK company

Published by arrangement with Image, an imprint of Random House, a division of
Penguin Random House LLC. First published in the United States in 2022

Originally published in Italy as Il Vangelo della domenica: Commentato dal Santo Padre
Ciclo domenicale e festive anno A by Mondadori Libri S.p.A.,/Rizzoli, Milan, in 2019
All rights reserved

A CIP catalogue record for this title is available from the British Library

Hardback ISBN 978 1 399 80346 5
eBook ISBN 978 1 399 80348 9

Printed and bound in Great Britain by Clays Ltd, Elcograf S.p.A.

Hodder & Stoughton policy is to use papers that are natural, renewable and recyclable
products and made from wood grown in sustainable forests. The logging and manufacturing
processes are expected to conform to the environmental regulations of the country of origin.

Hodder & Stoughton Ltd
Carmelite House
50 Victoria Embankment
London EC4Y 0DZ

www.hodderfaith.com

Contents

Contents

Contents

Introduction

Today we begin a new series of catecheses, which will direct our gaze toward the "heart" of the Church, namely, the Eucharist. It is fundamental that we Christians clearly understand the value and significance of the Holy Mass, in order to live out our relationship with God ever more fully.

In the year 304, during the Diocletianic Persecution, a group of Christians from North Africa were surprised by soldiers as they were celebrating Mass in a house, and were arrested. In the interrogation, the Roman proconsul asked them why they had done so, knowing that it was absolutely prohibited. They responded: "Without Sunday we cannot live," which meant: if we cannot celebrate the Eucharist, we cannot live; our Christian life would die.

Those Christians from North Africa were killed because they were celebrating the Eucharist. They gave witness that one can renounce earthly life for the Eucharist, because it gives us eternal life, making us participants in Christ's victory over death. This witness challenges us all and calls for a response to what it means for each of us to partake in the Sacrifice of Mass and approach the Lord's table.

The Eucharist is a wondrous event in which Jesus Christ, our life, makes himself present. Participating in the Mass "is truly living again the redemptive Passion and death of Our Lord. It is a visible manifestation. The Lord makes himself present on the altar to be offered to the Father for the salvation of the world" (*Homily at the Domus Sanctae Marthae*, February 10, 2014).

The Lord is there with us, present. But so often when we go to Mass, we look at things around us and talk among ourselves, all while the priest is celebrating the Eucharist . . . and we do not celebrate close to him.

But it is the Lord! He is there, present! If today the President of the Republic were to come, or some very important world personage, it is certain that we would all try to gather close to him, that we would want to greet him. So think: when you go to Mass, the Lord is there! And yet you get distracted. Remember, it is the Lord! We have to think about this.

"Father, it's that the Masses are dull," you say.

"But what are you saying, that the Lord is dull?"

"No, no," you respond. "Not the Mass, the priests."

"Ah, may the priests convert, but it is the Lord who is there!

"Participating in Mass is living again the redemptive Passion and death of Our Lord." Do you understand? Do not forget it.

Now let us try asking ourselves a few simple questions. For example, why do we make the sign of the Cross and perform the Penitential Rite at the beginning of Mass? Here, I would like to add an important side note: Have you seen how children make the sign of the Cross? No one knows what they are doing, whether it is the sign of the Cross or an outline. They do this [*gesturing*]. Children must be taught how to make the sign of the Cross properly. This is how the Mass begins; this is how life begins; this is how the day begins. This means that we are redeemed by the Lord's Cross. Watch the children and teach them how to make the sign of the Cross properly.

And those readings, during Mass, why are they there? Why are there three readings on Sunday and two on the other days? Why are they read? What do the readings at Mass mean? What is their purpose? Or why does the priest presiding at the celebration say at a certain point: "Lift up our hearts"? He does not say: "Lift up your cell phones to take a photo"! No, that's bad! I tell you, it makes me sad when I am celebrating here in Saint Peter's Square or in the Basilica to see many cell phones lifted up, not only by the faithful but also by some priests and even bishops! But please! Mass is not a spectacle. It is a time to encounter the Passion and Resurrection of the Lord. This is why the priest says: "Lift up our hearts." What does this mean? Remember: no cell phones!

In order to get his message across, Christ also makes use of the words of the priest who, after the Gospel, gives the homily. Strongly recommended by the Second Vatican Council as part of the liturgy itself, the homily is not a trite discourse—nor a catechesis like the one I am giving now—nor is it a conference or a lesson. The homily is something else. What is the homily? It is taking up "once more the dialogue which the Lord has already established with his people," so it may find fulfillment in life. The authentic exegesis of the Gospel is our holy life! The Word of the Lord concludes its journey by becoming flesh in us, being translated into works, as happened in Mary and in the saints. The Word of the Lord enters through the ears, goes to the heart, and passes to the hands, to good deeds. And the homily also follows the Word of the Lord and also follows this path in order to help us, so that the Word of the Lord may go to the hands, by passing through the heart.

If at times there is reason for boredom because a homily is long or unfocused or unintelligible, at other times prejudice creates the obstacle. And the homilist must be aware that he is not doing something of his own, but is preaching, giving voice to Jesus; he is preaching the Word of Jesus. And the homily must be prepared well. It must be brief, short!

My brief reflections on the Sunday Gospel, drawn from the comments made during the Angelus and some homilies in recent years, are for all readers—so we may all live out what we learn in Sunday Mass.

May the Word of God reach our hearts, touch our lives, and transform us, so that we, like the first Christians, can say, "Without Sunday, we cannot live."

Reflections on the Sunday Gospel

A New Horizon

First Sunday of Advent

✝

Matthew 24:37–44

41 "Two women will be grinding at the mill; one will be taken, and one will be left. 42 Therefore, stay awake! For you do not know on which day your Lord will come. 43 Be sure of this: if the master of the house had known the hour of night when the thief was coming, he would have stayed awake and not let his house be broken into."

Today in the Church a new liturgical year begins, which is a new journey of faith for the People of God. And as always, we begin with Advent. The passage of the Gospel (Mt 24:37–44) introduces us to one of the most evocative themes of Advent: *the visit of the Lord to humanity*. The first visit—we all know—occurred with the Incarnation, Jesus' birth in the cave of Bethlehem; the second takes place in the present: the Lord visits us constantly, each day, walking alongside us and being a consoling presence; in the end, there will be the third, the last visit, which we proclaim each time that we recite the Creed: "He will come again in glory to judge the living and the dead." Today, the Lord speaks to us about this final visit, which will take place at the end of time, and he tells us where we will arrive on our journey.

The Word of God emphasizes the contrast between the normal unfolding of events, the everyday *routine,* and the unexpected coming of the Lord. Jesus says: "In [those] days before the flood, they were eating and drinking, marrying and giving in marriage, up to the day that Noah entered the ark. They did not know until the flood came and carried them all away" (vv. 38–39): so says Jesus. It always strikes a chord when we think about the hours which precede a great disaster: everyone is calm, and they go about their usual business without realizing that their lives are about to be turned upside down. Of course, the Gospel does not want to scare us, but to open our horizons to *another,* greater dimension, one which on the one hand puts into perspective everyday things, while at the same time making them precious, crucial. The relationship with the God-who-comes-to-visit-us gives every gesture, everything a different light, a substance, a symbolic value.

From this perspective there also comes an invitation to *sobriety,* to not be controlled by the things of this world, by material reality, but rather to govern them. If, by contrast, we allow ourselves to be influenced and overpowered by these things, we cannot perceive that there is something very important: our final encounter with the Lord. This is important. That encounter. And everyday matters must have this horizon, and must be directed to that horizon: this encounter with the Lord, who comes for us. In that moment, as the Gospel says, "Two men will be out in the field; one will be taken and one will be left" (v. 40). It is an invitation to be vigilant, because in not knowing when he will come, we need to be ever ready to leave.

In this season of Advent, we are called to expand the horizons of our hearts, to be amazed by the life which presents itself each day with newness. In order to do this, we must learn to not depend on our own certainties, on our own established strategies, because the Lord comes at a time that we do not imagine. He comes to bring us into a more beautiful and grand dimension.

Readings from the Fathers of the Church

Saint Augustine,
Let us love and not fear him who will come

What then will the Christian do? He will make use of the world, but not become the world's slave. What does that mean? In spite of having things, he will behave as if he did not have them. This is what the apostle Paul says: "The world in its present form is passing away. I should like you to be free of anxieties" (1 Cor 7:31–32).

He who has no worries is serene in waiting for the coming of the Lord. In fact, what sort of love do we have for Christ if we are afraid of his coming? And are we not ashamed of this, brothers? We love him, and we are afraid of his coming. But do we truly love him? Or is it, perhaps, that we love Christ less than our sins? Well then, let us hate sin, and love him who will come to punish sin! Whether we like it or not, he will come. If he does not come immediately, it does not mean that he will never come. He will certainly come, and when you least expect it.

If you want to find him full of mercy, be merciful yourself before he comes. If someone has slighted you, forgive him. If you have something in surplus, give it to your neighbor. Whose, in fact, are the things that you give? Are they not, perhaps, his things? If you were to give your own garment, you would be making an optional donation; but since you give the garment you got from him, you make nothing but a restitution. What in fact do you have that you have not received (cf. 1 Cor 4:7)? These, then, are the victims most pleasing to God: compassion, humility, confession, peace, charity. Let us bring these offerings to the altar and we will wait calmly for the coming of the judge, who will judge the world according to justice and the peoples according to his truth (cf. Ps 9:9).

A Big "Yes"

The Immaculate Conception
of the Blessed Virgin Mary

☩

Luke 1:26–38

34 "How can this be, since I have no relations with a man?"
35 And the angel said to her in reply, "The holy Spirit will
come upon you, and the power of the Most High will over-
shadow you. Therefore the child to be born will be called
holy, the Son of God. 36 And behold, Elizabeth, your relative, has also conceived a son in her old age, and this is the
sixth month for her who was called barren; 37 for nothing
will be impossible for God." 38 Mary said, "Behold, I am the
handmaid of the Lord. May it be done to me according to
your word." Then the angel departed from her.

Today's Gospel of the Immaculate Conception of the
Blessed Virgin Mary presents a crucial point in the history of the relationship between man and God, leading us to
the origin of good and evil. This is when God comes to live
among us, becoming man like us.

And this was made possible through a great "yes"—that of
the sin was the "no"; this is the "yes," it is a great "yes"—that

of Mary at the moment of the Annunciation. Because of this "yes," Jesus began his journey along the path of humanity; he began it in Mary, spending the first months of life in his Mother's womb. He did not appear as a man, grown and strong, but he followed the journey of a human being. He was made equal to us in every way, except for one thing, that "no." Except for sin. For this reason, he chose Mary, the only creature without sin, immaculate. In the Gospel, with one word only, she is called "full of grace" (Lk 1:28), that is, filled with grace. It means that, in her, full of grace from the start, there is no space for sin. And when we turn to her, we too recognize this beauty: we invoke her, "full of grace," without a shadow of evil.

Mary responds to God's proposal by saying: "Behold, I am the handmaid of the Lord" (v. 38). She does not say: "Well, this time I will do God's will; I will make myself available, then I will see . . ." No. Hers is a full, total "yes," for her entire life, without conditions. And just as the original "no" closed the passage between man and God, so Mary's "yes" opened the path to God among us. It is the most important "yes" in history, the humble "yes" that reverses the prideful original "no," the faithful "yes" that heals disobedience, the willing "yes" that overturns the vanity of sin.

For each of us too, there is a history of salvation made up of yeses and nos. Sometimes, though, we are experts in the halfhearted "yes": we are good at pretending not to understand what God wants and what our conscience suggests. We are also crafty. And so as not to say a true "no" to God, we say: "Sorry, I can't"; "Not today, I think tomorrow." "Tomorrow

I'll be better; tomorrow I will pray, I will do good tomorrow." This cunning leads us away from the "yes." It distances us from God and leads us to "no," to the sinful "no," to the "no" of mediocrity: the famous "yes, but . . ."; "yes, Lord, but . . ." In this way we close the door to goodness, and evil takes advantage of these omitted yeses. Each of us has a collection of them within. Think about it: we will find many omitted yeses.

Instead, every complete "yes" to God gives rise to a new story. To say "yes" to God is truly "original." It is the origin, not the sin, that makes us old on the inside. Have you thought about this, that sin makes us old on the inside? It makes us grow old quickly! Every "yes" to God gives rise to stories of salvation for us and for others. Like Mary with her own "yes."

In this Advent journey, God wishes to visit us and awaits our "yes." Let's think: *I, today, what "yes" must I say to God?* Let's think about it; it will do us good. And we will find the Lord's voice in God, who asks something of us: a step forward. "I believe in you; I hope in you. I love you; be it done to me according to your good will." This is the "yes."

With generosity and trust, like Mary, let us say today, each of us, this personal "yes" to God.

Readings from the Fathers of the Church

Saint Augustine,
The first disciple of Christ

"For whoever does the will of my heavenly Father is my brother, and sister, and mother" (Mt 12:50). Was not one who did the Father's will the Virgin Mary, who through faith believed, through faith conceived, was chosen so that from her salvation should be born for us among men, and was created by Christ before Christ was created in her womb? Holy Mary did the Father's will and did it to the full; and thus it is worth more for Mary to have been a disciple rather than the mother of Christ. It is worth more, it is a more blessed prerogative to have been a disciple rather than the mother of Christ. Mary was blessed because before bringing him forth she carried in her womb the Teacher. [. . .]

"Rather, blessed are those who hear the word of God and observe it" (Lk 11:28). So this is why Mary too was blessed, because she listened to the word of God and put it into practice. She kept the truth in her mind more than the flesh in her womb. The truth is Christ, the flesh is Christ: Christ truth in the mind of Mary, Christ flesh in the womb of Mary; there is more worth in that which is in the mind than in that which is carried in the womb. [. . .]

Dearly beloved, consider what you yourselves are: you too are members of Christ and the body of Christ. Pay attention to how you are that which Christ says: "Here are my mother and my brothers" (Mt 12:49). How can you be Christ's mother? "Whoever does the will of my heavenly Father is my brother, and sister, and mother" (cf. Mt 12:50).

True Joy

Third Sunday of Advent

✝

Matthew 11:2–11

2 When John heard in prison of the works of the Messiah, he sent his disciples to him 3 with this question, "Are you the one who is to come, or should we look for another?" 4 Jesus said to them in reply, "Go and tell John what you hear and see: 5 the blind regain their sight, the lame walk, lepers are cleansed, the deaf hear, the dead are raised, and the poor have the good news proclaimed to them. 6 And blessed is the one who takes no offense at me."

Today we celebrate the Third Sunday of Advent, which is characterized by Saint Paul's invitation: "Rejoice in the Lord always; again, I will say, Rejoice. . . . The Lord is at hand" (Phil 4:4–6). It is not a superficial or purely emotional cheerfulness that the apostle exhorts, nor is it the cheerfulness of worldliness or of consumerism. No, it is not that, but rather, it entails a more authentic joy, the taste of which we are called to rediscover. The taste of true joy. It is a joy that touches our innermost being, as we await Jesus, who has already come to bring salvation to the world, the promised Messiah, born in Bethlehem of the Virgin Mary.

In today's Gospel, the imprisoned John the Baptist sends his disciples to ask Jesus a very clear question: "Are you the one who is to come, or should we look for another?" (Mt 11:3). John was in a moment of darkness; he was anxiously awaiting the Messiah and used colorful language to describe him in his preaching as a judge who would finally inaugurate the Kingdom of God and purify his people, rewarding the good and punishing the bad. John preached in this way: "Even now the ax lies at the root of the trees. Therefore every tree that does not bear good fruit will be cut down and thrown into the fire" (Mt 3:10). Now that Jesus has begun his public mission in a different manner, John suffers because he is in a two-fold darkness: the darkness of his prison cell, and the darkness of heart. He does not understand this manner of Jesus, and he wants to know if he is really the Messiah, or if he must await someone else.

And what does Jesus say to these messengers? "The blind regain their sight, the lame walk, lepers are cleansed, the deaf hear, the dead are raised" (Mt 11:5).

They are not words, but are facts which demonstrate how salvation, brought by Jesus, seizes the human being and re-generates him. God has entered history in order to free us from the slavery of sin; he set his tent in our midst in order to share our existence, to heal our lesions, to bind our wounds, and to give us new life. Joy is the fruit of this intervention of God's salvation and love.

We are called to let ourselves be drawn in by the feeling of exultation. But a Christian who isn't joyful is a Christian who is lacking something, or else is not a Christian! It is heartfelt joy, the joy within which leads us forth and gives us courage. The Lord comes, he comes into our life as a liberator; he comes to free us from all forms of interior and exterior slavery. It is he who shows us the path of faithfulness, of patience, and of perseverance because, upon his return, our joy will be overflowing. Christmas is near, the signs of his approach are evident along our streets and in our houses; here too, in Saint Peter's Square, the nativity scene has been set up with the tree beside it. These outward signs invite us to welcome the Lord, who always comes and knocks at our door, knocks at our heart, in order to draw near to us; he invites us to recognize his footsteps among the brothers and sisters who pass beside us, especially the weakest and most needy.

Today we are called to rejoice for the imminent coming of our Redeemer; and we are called to share this joy with others, giving comfort and hope to the poor, the sick, and to people who are lonely and unhappy.

May the Virgin Mary, the "handmaid of the Lord," help us to hear God's voice in prayer and to serve him with compassion in our brothers, so as to be prepared for the Christmas appointment, preparing our hearts to welcome Jesus.

Readings from the Fathers of the Church

Saint Jerome,
From everyday toil to true joy

"For they will hardly dwell on the shortness of life, because God lets them busy themselves with the joy of their heart" (Eccl 5:19). The Lord certainly grants joy to the heart of the wise man; he will not be in sadness; he will not be tormented by anxiety, absorbed as he is by the present gladness and pleasure. The concept is expressed better by Saint Paul when he speaks of a spiritual food and drink granted by God (cf. 1 Cor 10:3) and glimpses the goodness of his every effort in being able to contemplate those true goods through the toil of work. This is our part, which brings us joy even in the toil of work, because as much as it is good to work, nevertheless until Christ is manifested in our life, we have not yet attained a complete good. In this sense not even God will think too much of the days of our life. In this sense the occupation spoken of is to be understood as the spiritual occupation that brings true joy. [. . .]

The Christian man, on closer inspection, knows the heavenly Scriptures, and all the efforts of his words and of his soul employ him until he is full of that which he always desires to learn. He has this much more than the fool: the fact of feeling himself poor, like that poor man who in the Gospel is called blessed. Feeling himself poor, he hastens to embrace those things which are vital for him, while still traveling the hard and narrow path that leads to that which gives life. He is poor in wicked works and knows where to dwell: in Christ, who is the life.

God Near to Us

Fourth Sunday of Advent

+

Matthew 1:18–24

18 Now this is how the birth of Jesus Christ came about. When his mother Mary was betrothed to Joseph, but before they lived together, she was found with child through the holy Spirit. 19 Joseph her husband, since he was a righteous man, yet unwilling to expose her to shame, decided to divorce her quietly. 20 Such was his intention when, behold, the angel of the Lord appeared to him in a dream and said, "Joseph, son of David, do not be afraid to take Mary your wife into your home. For it is through the holy Spirit that this child has been conceived in her. 21 She will bear a son and you are to name him Jesus, because he will save his people from their sins."

The liturgy for today, the Fourth and last Sunday of Advent, is characterized by the theme of closeness, God's closeness to humanity. The Gospel passage (Mt 1:18–24) shows us two people, the two people who, more than anyone else, were involved in this mystery of love: the Virgin Mary and her husband, Joseph. A mystery of love, the mystery of God's closeness to humanity.

Mary is presented in the light of the prophet who says: "Behold, the virgin shall be with child and bear a son" (v. 23). Matthew the Evangelist recognizes that this happened in Mary, who conceived Jesus through the Holy Spirit (cf. v. 18). The Son of God "comes" into her womb in order to become man, and she welcomes him. Thus, in a unique way, God drew near to mankind, taking on flesh through a woman: God drew near to us and took on flesh through a woman.

To us too, in a different way, God draws near with his grace in order to enter our life and offer us the gift of his Son. What do we do? Do we welcome him, let him draw near, or do we reject him, push him away? As Mary, freely offering herself to the Lord of history, allowed him to change the destiny of mankind, so too can we, by welcoming Jesus and seeking to follow him each day, cooperate in his salvific plan for us and for the world. Mary thus appears to us as a model to look to and upon whose support we can count in our search for God, in our closeness to God, in thus allowing God to draw close to us and in our commitment to build the culture of love.

The other protagonist of today's Gospel is Saint Joseph. The Evangelist highlights that alone, Joseph cannot explain to himself the event which he sees taking place before his eyes, namely, Mary's pregnancy. Just then, in that moment of doubt, even anguish, God approaches him—him too— through his messenger and [Joseph] is enlightened about the nature of this maternity: "it is through the holy Spirit that this child has been conceived in her" (cf. v. 20). Thus, in facing this extraordinary event, which surely gave rise to many questions in his heart, he trusts totally in God, who has drawn near to him, and after his invitation, does not repudiate his betrothed, but takes her to him and takes Mary to wife. In accepting Mary, Joseph knowingly and lovingly receives him who has been conceived in her through the wondrous work of God, for whom nothing is impossible. Joseph, a just and humble man (cf. v. 19), teaches us to always trust in God, who draws near to us: when God approaches us, we must entrust ourselves to him. Joseph teaches us to allow ourselves to be guided by him with willing obedience.

These two figures, Mary and Joseph, who were the first to welcome Jesus through faith, introduce us to the mystery of Christmas. Mary helps us to assume an attitude of openness in order to welcome the Son of God into our concrete life, in our flesh. Joseph spurs us to always seek God's will and to follow it with full trust. Both allow God to draw near to them. With them, we walk together toward Bethlehem.

And to God who draws near, do I open the door—to the Lord—when I sense an interior inspiration, when I hear him ask me to do something more for others, when he calls me to pray? God-with-us, God who draws near. This message of hope, which is fulfilled at Christmas, leads to fulfillment of the expectation of God in each one of us too, in all the Church, and in the many little ones whom the world scorns, but whom God also loves and to whom God draws near.

Readings from the Fathers of the Church

Saint Augustine,
Loving will bring God near to you

"The Lord is on high, but cares for the lowly and knows the proud from afar" (Ps 138:6). And how does he look at us? "The Lord is close to the brokenhearted" (Ps 34:19). So do not go looking for a high summit on which you think you will be closer to God. If you lift yourself up, he withdraws from you; if instead you lower yourself, he stoops down to you. The publican stood back, and because of this God drew near to him more easily; and he did not dare raise his eyes to heaven (cf. Lk 18:13), but he already possessed within himself the one who had made heaven.

So how will we rejoice in the Lord, if the Lord is so far from us? But you must act in such a way that he may not withdraw; you are the one who keeps him at a distance. Love, and he will draw near; love, and he will dwell in you. "The Lord is near. Have no anxiety at all" (Phil 4:5–6). Do you want to see how true it is that he is with you if you love? God is charity (1 Jn 4:8). Why do the images in your mind flutter about here and there, and you wonder: "Whatever could God be? Whatever could God be like?" All that you can imagine he is not; all that you can embrace with your thought he is not: because all that he is cannot be embraced with thought. But look, just to get a little taste, God is charity. "And charity, what is that?" you will say to me. Charity is the power with which we love.

Feel the Father's Love with Your Hand

The Nativity of the Lord

✝

John 1:9–14

9 The true light, which enlightens everyone, was coming into the world. 10 He was in the world, and the world came to be through him, but the world did not know him. . . . 14 And the Word became flesh and made his dwelling among us, and we saw his glory, the glory as of the Father's only Son, full of grace and truth.

The liturgy today presents to us the Prologue of the Gospel of Saint John (1:9–14), in which it is proclaimed that "the Word"—that is, the creative Word of God—"became flesh and made his dwelling among us" (v. 14). In other words, that Word, which dwells in heaven in the dimension of God, came upon the earth so that we should hear it and we could know and physically touch the Love of the Father. The Word of God is his Only Begotten Son, having become man, full of love and devotion (cf. v. 14); it is Jesus himself.

The Evangelist does not hide the dramatic nature of the

Incarnation of the Son of God, emphasizing that the gift of God's love is marked by mankind's failure to receive it. The Word is the light, yet mankind preferred darkness; the Word came among his own, but they received him not (cf. vv. 9–10). They closed the door in the face of God's Son. It is the mystery of evil that undermines our life too, and it requires vigilance and attention on our part so that it does not prevail.

The Book of Genesis offers a nice phrase that lets us understand this: it says that sin is "crouching at the door" (cf. 4:7). Woe to us should we let it enter, lest sin would close our door to anyone else. Instead we are called to open wide the door of our heart to the Word of God, to Jesus, in order to become his children in this way.

On this Christmas Day, this solemn beginning of the Gospel of Saint John was proclaimed; today it is offered to us once again. It is the invitation of the Holy Mother Church to welcome this Word of salvation, this mystery of light. If we welcome him, if we welcome Jesus, we will grow in the knowledge and the love of the Lord; we will learn to be merciful like him. Particularly in this Holy Year of Mercy, let us allow the Gospel to become ever more incarnate in our lives as well. Approaching the Gospel, contemplating it, and embodying it in daily life is the best way to come to know Jesus and to bring him to others. This is the vocation and the joy of every baptized person: to reveal and give Jesus to others; but in order to do this we must know him and bear him within us, as the Lord of our life. He protects us from the evil one, from the devil, who is always lurking at our door, at our heart, and wants to get in.

**With a renewed impetus of filial abandon, let us entrust
ourselves once again to Mary: may we contemplate her gentle image as the Mother of Jesus and our Mother in the nativity scene during these days.**

Readings from the Fathers of the Church

Saint Andrew of Crete,
Enveloped in light

He is coming who is present in every place and fills all things.
He is coming to accomplish in you the salvation of all. He is
coming who did not come to call the just, but sinners to repentance (cf. Mt 9:13), to call them back from the paths of
sin. So do not be afraid. There is a God in your midst, you will
not be shaken (cf. Dt 7:21). Welcome him with open arms.
Receive him who on his palms has marked the borders of your
walls, and has laid your foundations with his own hands.

Receive him who within himself received all that which belongs to human nature, except for sin. Be glad, O city of Zion,
our mother, "celebrate your festivals" (Na 2:1). Glorify him
who out of his great mercy is coming to us by means of you.
But let your heart rejoice as well, daughter of Jerusalem, break
into song, set your feet to dancing. Clothe yourself in light,
"arise! Shine," let us cry out with Isaiah, "for your light has
come, the glory of the Lord has dawned upon you" (Is 60:1).

But what light? That which enlightens every man who
comes into the world (cf. Jn 1:9). I say the eternal light, the
timeless light that has appeared in time. The light that has
been manifested in the flesh, light that by its nature is con-

cealed. The light that enveloped the shepherds and was the guide for the Magi on their journey. The light that was in the world from the beginning, and by means of which the world was made, that world which did not know it. The light that came among his people, and that his own did not receive.

Martyrs, the Ones Who Witness the Light of Truth

Feast of St. Stephen, Protomartyr

┿

Matthew 10:17–22

17 But beware of people, for they will hand you over to courts and scourge you in their synagogues, 18 and you will be led before governors and kings for my sake as a witness before them and the pagans. 19 When they hand you over, do not worry about how you are to speak or what you are to say. You will be given at that moment what you are to say. 20 For it will not be you who speak but the Spirit of your Father speaking through you.

The joy of Christmas fills our hearts today too, as the liturgy involves us in celebrating the martyrdom of Saint Stephen, the First Martyr, inviting us to reflect on the witness that he gave us with his sacrifice. It is precisely the glorious witness of Christian martyrdom, suffered for love of Christ; the martyrdom which continues to be present in the history of the Church, from Stephen up to our time.

Today's Gospel (cf. Mt 10:17–22) told us of this witness.

Jesus forewarns the disciples of the rejection and persecution they will encounter: "you will be hated by all because of my name" (v. 22). But why does the world persecute Christians? The world hates Christians for the same reason that they hated Jesus: because he brought the light of God, and the world prefers darkness so as to hide its evil works. Let us recall that Jesus himself, at the Last Supper, prayed that the Father might protect us from the wicked worldly spirit. There is opposition between the Gospel and this worldly mentality. Following Jesus means following his light, which was kindled in the night of Bethlehem, and abandoning worldly obscurity.

The protomartyr Stephen, full of the Holy Spirit, was stoned because he professed his faith in Jesus Christ, the Son of God. The Only Begotten Son who comes into the world invites every believer to choose the way of light and life. This is the meaning of his coming among us. Loving the Lord and obeying his voice, the deacon Stephen chose Christ, Life and Light for all mankind. By choosing truth, he became at the same time a victim of the inexplicable iniquity present in the world. But in Christ, Stephen triumphed!

Today too, in order to bear witness to light and to truth, the Church experiences, in different places, harsh persecution, up to the supreme sacrifice of martyrdom. How many of our brothers and sisters in faith endure abuse and violence, and are hated because of Jesus! I shall tell you something: today's martyrs are even more numerous than those of the first centuries. When we read the history of the first centuries, here in Rome, we read of so much cruelty toward Christians. I tell you: there is the same cruelty today, and to a greater extent, toward Christians. Today we should think of those who are suffering from persecution, and be close to them with our affection, our prayers, and also our tears. Yesterday, Christmas Day, Christians persecuted in Iraq celebrated Christmas in their destroyed cathedral: it is an example of faithfulness to the Gospel. In spite of the trials and dangers, they courageously witness their belonging to Christ and live the Gospel by committing themselves in favor of the least, of the most neglected, doing good to all without distinction; in this way they witness to charity in truth.

In making room in our heart for the Son of God who gives himself to us at Christmas, let us joyfully and courageously renew the will to follow him faithfully, as the only guide, by continuing to live according to the Gospel attitude and rejecting the mentality of those who dominate this world.

Let us raise our prayers to the Virgin Mary, Mother of God and Queen of Martyrs, that she may guide us and always sustain us on our journey in following Jesus Christ, whom we contemplate in the grotto of the nativity and who is the faithful Witness of God the Father.

Readings from the Fathers of the Church

Saint Caesarius of Arles,
We can imitate the martyrs

The holy martyrs, dearest brothers, were eager to love even their enemies: what share with them can they have who at times do not even return the affection of their friends?

So let us not be lazy, dearest brothers, in imitating the holy martyrs as much as we can, so that through their merits and prayers we may deserve to be absolved from every sin.

But some say: "And who is able to imitate the holy martyrs?" Even if not in everything, nevertheless in many things, with God's help, we can and should imitate them.

You are not able to bear the flames? You can still keep away from lust. You are not able to endure the iron that rends? Despise greed, which drives you to wrongful commerce and to ungodly profits. In fact, if you are defeated by pleasures, how will you make it through harsher trials?

Even peace has its martyrs. In fact, overcoming anger, shunning envy like a serpent's venom, rejecting pride, driving hatred from the heart, curbing the desire for excessive food and drink, not giving in to drunkenness, all this is a large part of martyrdom.

Whenever and wherever you see that a just cause is in danger, if you bear witness in its favor, you are a martyr. And since Christ is justice and truth, wherever justice or truth or chastity is threatened, if you defend them with all your might, you will receive the recompense of the martyrs. And since the Greek word "martyr" means "witness," whoever bears witness to the truth will undoubtedly be a martyr of Christ, who is the truth.

Communities of Love and Reconciliation

The Holy Family of Jesus, Mary and Joseph

✝

Matthew 2:13–15, 19–23

13 When they had departed, behold, the angel of the Lord appeared to Joseph in a dream and said, "Rise, take the child and his mother, flee to Egypt, and stay there until I tell you. Herod is going to search for the child to destroy him." 14 Joseph rose and took the child and his mother by night and departed for Egypt. 15 He stayed there until the death of Herod, that what the Lord had said through the prophet might be fulfilled, "Out of Egypt I called my son." [. . .] 19 When Herod had died, behold, the angel of the Lord appeared in a dream to Joseph in Egypt 20 and said, "Rise, take the child and his mother and go to the land of Israel, for those who sought the child's life are dead." 21 He rose, took the child and his mother, and went to the land of Israel. 22 But when he heard that Archelaus was ruling over Judea in place of his father Herod, he was afraid to go back there. And because he had been warned in a dream, he departed for the region of Galilee. 23 He went and dwelt in a town called Nazareth, so that what had been spoken through the prophets might be fulfilled, "He shall be called a Nazarene."

On this first Sunday after Christmas, the liturgy invites us to celebrate the Feast of the Sacred Family of Nazareth. Indeed, every nativity scene shows us Jesus together with Our Lady and Saint Joseph in the grotto of Bethlehem. God wanted to be born into a human family, he wanted to have a mother and father like us.

And today the Gospel presents the Sacred Family to us on the sorrowful road of exile, seeking refuge in Egypt. Joseph, Mary, and Jesus experienced the tragic fate of refugees, which is marked by fear, uncertainty, and unease (Mt 2:13-15, 19-23). Unfortunately, in our own time, millions of families can identify with this sad reality. Almost every day the television and newspapers carry news of refugees fleeing from hunger, war, and other grave dangers, in search of security and a dignified life for themselves and for their families.

In distant lands, even when they find work, refugees and immigrants do not always find a true welcome, respect, and appreciation for the values they bring. Their legitimate expectations collide with complex and difficult situations which at times seem insurmountable. Therefore, as we fix our gaze on the Sacred Family of Nazareth as they were forced to become refugees, let us think of the tragedy of those migrants and refugees who are victims of rejection and exploitation, who are victims of human trafficking and of slave labor. But let us also think of the other "exiles": I would call them "hidden exiles," those exiles who can be found within their own families: the elderly, for example, who are sometimes treated as a burdensome presence. I often think that a good indicator for knowing how a family is doing is seeing how their children and the elderly are treated.

Jesus wanted to belong to a family who experienced these hardships, so that no one would feel excluded from the loving closeness of God. The flight into Egypt caused by Herod's threat shows us that God is present where man is in danger, where man is suffering, where he is fleeing, where he experiences rejection and abandonment; God is also present where man dreams, where he hopes to return in freedom to his homeland, and plans and chooses life for his family and dignity for himself and his loved ones.

Today our gaze on the Sacred Family lets us also be drawn into the simplicity of the life they led in Nazareth. It is an example that does our families great good, helping them increasingly to become communities of love and reconciliation, in which tenderness, mutual help, and mutual forgiveness are experienced. Let us remember the three key phrases for living in peace and joy in the family: "may I," "thank you," and "sorry." In our family, when we are not intrusive and ask "may I," in our family when we are not selfish and learn to say "thank you," and when in a family one realizes he has done something wrong and knows how to say "sorry," in that family there is peace and joy.

I would also like to encourage families to become aware of the importance they have in the Church and in society. The proclamation of the Gospel, in fact, first passes through the family to reach the various spheres of daily life.

Let us fervently call upon Mary Most Holy, the Mother of
Jesus and our Mother, and Saint Joseph, her spouse. Let us
ask them to enlighten, comfort, and guide every family in
the world, so that they may fulfill with dignity and peace
the mission which God has entrusted to them.

Readings from the Fathers of the Church

Saint Ambrose,
Love your parents as Christ loved his

Honor your parents, because the Son of God honored his;
you have read, in fact: "And [he] was obedient to them" (Lk
2:51). If God was obedient to two poor servants, how should
you behave with your parents? Christ honored Joseph and
Mary not on account of a debt of nature, but on account of a
duty of piety, and moreover he honored God his Father in the
way no one else could ever have done, to the point of being
"obedient unto death" (Phil 2:8); so honor your parents as
well.

Honor, however, consists not only in manifestations of respect but also in generosity. [. . .] Honor in fact means giving
help according to the other's merits. Support your father, support your mother. And even when you support your mother
you will never make up for the suffering, you will never repay
the torment she bore for you; you will not repay the acts of
love with which she carried you in her womb; you will not
repay the nourishment that she gave you, gently pressing her
breasts to your lips with the tenderness of affection; you will
not repay the hunger that she suffered for you, when she did

not want to eat anything that could harm you, or touch anything that would taint her milk. For you she fasted, for you she ate, for you she refused food even though she wanted it, for you she ate food that she did not like, for you she lost sleep, for you she wept. And will you allow her to live in want? O son, what a terrible judgment you are going to meet, if you do not support her who gave birth to you! To her you owe what you have because you owe what you are.

His Closeness Never Fades

Second Sunday after the Nativity

✝

John 1:1–18

11 He came to what was his own, but his own people did not accept him. 12 But to those who did accept him he gave power to become children of God, to those who believe in his name, 13 who were born not by natural generation nor by human choice nor by a man's decision but of God. 14 And the Word became flesh and made his dwelling among us, and we saw his glory, the glory as of the Father's only Son, full of grace and truth.

Once again, the liturgy this Sunday sets before us, in the Prologue of the Gospel of Saint John, the most profound significance of the birth of Jesus. He is the Word of God, who became man and pitched his "tent," his dwelling, among men. The Evangelist writes: "And the Word became flesh and made his dwelling among us" (Jn 1:14). These words, which never cease to amaze us, contain the whole of Christianity! God became mortal, fragile like us; he shared in our human condition, except for sin, but he took our sins upon himself, as though they were his own. He entered into our history; he became fully God-with-us! The birth of Jesus, then, shows us that God wanted to unite himself to every man and every woman, to every one of us, to communicate to us his life and his joy.

Thus, God is God-with-us, God who loves us, God who walks with us. This is the message of Christmas: The Word became flesh. Thus, Christmas reveals to us the immense love that God has for humanity. From this too derives our enthusiasm, our hope as Christians, that in our poverty we may know that we are loved, that we have been visited, that we are accompanied by God; and we look upon the world and on history as a place in which we walk together with him among us toward a new heaven and a new earth. With the birth of Jesus, a new promise is born, a new world comes into being, but also a world that can be ever renewed. God is always present to stir up new men, to purify the world of the sin that makes it grow old, from the sin that corrupts it. However much human history and the personal story of each of us may be marked by difficulty and weakness, faith in the Incarnation tells us that God is in solidarity with mankind and with human history. This closeness of God to man, to every man and woman, to each one of us, is a gift that never fades! He is with us! He is God-with-us! Behold the glad tidings of Christmas: the divine light that filled the hearts of the Virgin Mary and Saint Joseph, and guided the footsteps of the shepherds and the Magi, shines today too for us.

In the mystery of the Incarnation of the Son of God there is also an aspect that is connected to human freedom, to the freedom of each one of us. Indeed, the Word of God pitched his tent among us, sinners who are in need of mercy. And we all must hasten to receive the grace that he offers us. Instead, the Gospel of Saint John continues, "his own people did not accept him" (v. 11). We reject him too many times, we prefer to remain closed in our errors and the anxiety of our sins. But Jesus does not desist and never ceases to offer himself and his grace, which saves us! Jesus is patient, Jesus knows how to wait, he waits for us always. This is a message of hope, a message of salvation, ancient and ever new. And we are called to witness with joy this message of the Gospel of life, the Gospel of light, of hope and of love. For Jesus' message is this: life, light, hope, and love.

May Mary, the Mother of God and our tender Mother, support us always, that we may remain faithful to our Christian vocation and be able to realize the aspiration for justice and peace that we carry within us at the start of this new year.

Readings from the Fathers of the Church

Pseudo-Hippolytus, Christ accepted our suffering

We know that the Word received a body from a Virgin and put on the old man in order to shape him anew. [. . .]

But to keep from being seen as different from us, he subjected himself to toil, he was willing to bear hunger, he did not refuse to feel thirst, he had need of rest and sleep, he did not protest in his Passion, he became obedient unto death and made manifest the Resurrection, offering as the first fruits, in all these actions, his humanity, so that when you are in tribulation you may not lose heart, but in seeing that your nature as man corresponds with his own you may anticipate that which has been granted [. . .] to him.

In fact, Christ is the God above all things, he who arranged to wash men's sins away, making new the old man whom he had called "in his image" (cf. Gn 1:26) from the beginning, manifesting through the "likeness" his love for you, if you will obey his venerable commandments. If you become a good imitator of him who is good, you will be, as one who is alike, honored by him. In fact, God lacks nothing, even if he makes you god, to his glory.

Follow the Gentle Light

The Epiphany of the Lord

+

Matthew 2:1–12

1 When Jesus was born in Bethlehem of Judea, in the days of King Herod, behold, magi from the east arrived in Jerusalem, 2 saying, "Where is the newborn king of the Jews? We saw his star at its rising and have come to do him homage." [. . .] 10 They were overjoyed at seeing the star, 11 and on entering the house they saw the child with Mary his mother. They prostrated themselves and did him homage. Then they opened their treasures and offered him gifts of gold, frankincense, and myrrh. 12 And having been warned in a dream not to return to Herod, they departed for their country by another way.

Today we are celebrating the Epiphany of the Lord, which is the manifestation of Jesus who shines as a light for all peoples. A symbol of this light, which shines in the world and seeks to enlighten the life of each one of us, is the star that guided the Magi to Bethlehem. The Gospel says that they had "[seen] his star at its rising" (Mt 2:2) and they chose to follow it: they chose to be guided by the star of Jesus.

In our life too there are several stars, lights that twinkle and guide. It is up to us to choose which ones to follow. For example, there are flashing lights that come and go, like the small pleasures of life: though they may be good, they are not enough, because they do not last long and they do not leave the peace we seek. Then there is the dazzling limelight of money and success, which promises everything, and at once. It is seductive, but with its intensity, blinds and causes dreams of glory to fade into the thickest darkness. The Magi, instead, invite us to follow a steady light, a gentle light that does not wane, because it is not of this world: it comes from heaven and shines . . . where? In the heart.

This true light is the light of the Lord, or rather, it is the Lord himself. He is our light: a light that does not dazzle, but accompanies and bestows a unique joy. This light is for everyone and it calls each one of us. In this way, we can hear addressed to us today's invitation from the prophet Isaiah: "Arise, shine" (60:1). So said Isaiah, prophesying this joy of today in Jerusalem, "Arise, shine." At the beginning of each day we can welcome this invitation: arise, shine, and follow today, among the many shooting stars in the world, the bright star of Jesus! Following it, we will experience the joy, as happened to the Magi, who "were overjoyed at seeing the star" (Mt 2:10); because where there is God, there is joy. Those who have encountered Jesus have experienced the miracle of light that pierces the darkness and know this light that illuminates and brightens. I would like, with great respect, to invite everyone not to fear this light and to open up to the Lord. Above all, I would like to say to those who have lost the strength to seek, who are tired, to those who, overwhelmed by the darkness of life, have extinguished this yearning: arise, take heart, the light of Jesus can overcome the deepest darkness. Arise, take heart!

And how do we find this divine light? We follow the example of the Magi, whom the Gospel describes as always on the move. He who wants the light, in fact, goes out of himself and seeks: he is not withdrawn, immobile, watching what is happening around him, but rather, he puts his own life at stake; he goes out of himself. Christian life is a continuous journey, made of hope, a quest; a journey which, like that of the Magi, continues even when the star momentarily disappears from view. On this journey there are also pitfalls that should be avoided: superficial and mundane gossip, which slows the pace; the paralyzing selfish whims; the pit of pessimism that ensnares hope. These obstacles hindered the scribes, of whom today's Gospel speaks. They knew where the light was, but did not move. When Herod asked them, "Where will the Messiah be born?" [They answered], "In Bethlehem!" (cf. Mt 2:4–5). They knew where, but did not budge. Their knowledge was vain: they knew many things, but it was useless, all in vain. It is not enough to know that God is born, if you do not celebrate Christmas in the heart with him. God is born, yes, but is he born in your heart? Is he born in my heart? Is he born in our hearts? And in this way, we will find him, as did the Magi, with Mary and Joseph in the stable.

The Magi went forth: having found the Child, they fell down and worshiped him. They did not just look at him, they did not just say a circumstantial prayer and leave. No indeed. They worshiped: they entered into a personal communion of love with Jesus. Then they offered him gold, frankincense, and myrrh, namely, their most precious belongings.

Let us learn from the Magi not to devote to Jesus only spare time and an occasional thought; otherwise we will not receive his light. Like the Magi, let us set out, let us shine as we follow the star of Jesus, and let us adore the Lord with all our hearts.

Readings from the Fathers of the Church

Origen,
A light more powerful than any spell

It therefore appears natural that even at the birth of Jesus, when "a multitude of the heavenly host," as Luke wrote (cf. Lk 2:13) and as I firmly believe, praised God and said: "Glory to God in the highest, and peace on earth to men of good will," the result of this was that the demons lost their power and their might, since their spell was broken and their mastery destroyed. These were destroyed not only by the angels who came down to the earthly regions for the birth of Jesus, but also by the very spirit of Jesus and by the divinity that was in him. Therefore the Magi, when they wanted to carry out their usual practices and were unable—those practices which they previously performed with formulas and divination—they sought out the cause of this, maintaining that it must be extraordinary, and in catching sight of that divine sign in the sky, they wanted to investigate its meaning. [. . .]

Then they conjectured that this man, whose birth was predicted by the appearance of the star, must have come into the world, and holding him to be more powerful than all the demons, and more powerful than the beings that usually appeared to them and had a certain magical power, they wanted to worship him. [. . .] They brought the gifts and offered them to him, who was (so to speak) a combination of God and mortal man; and these gifts were symbols, in that they offered him gold as king, myrrh as mortal, and incense as God; they offered these to him after they had learned the place of his birth. And then, since the savior of the human race was God, and higher than the angels who render aid to men, an angel returned that sentiment of piety which the Magi had shown by coming to worship Jesus, and warned them not to go to Herod, but to return to their country by a different way (cf. Mt 2:12).

The Attraction of Mildness and Humility

The Baptism of the Lord

✝

Matthew 3:13–17

13 Then Jesus came from Galilee to John at the Jordan to be baptized by him. 14 John tried to prevent him, saying, "I need to be baptized by you, and yet you are coming to me?" 15 Jesus said to him in reply, "Allow it now, for thus it is fitting for us to fulfill all righteousness." Then he allowed him. 16 After Jesus was baptized, he came up from the water and behold, the heavens were opened [for him], and he saw the Spirit of God descending like a dove [and] coming upon him. 17 And a voice came from the heavens, saying, "This is my beloved Son, with whom I am well pleased."

Today, in the Feast of the Baptism of Jesus, the Gospel (Mt 3:13–17) describes the scene which occurred at the river Jordan: Jesus too is in the midst of the penitent crowd that approaches John the Baptist to receive Baptism. He has stood in line. John would like to prevent him from [being baptized], saying: "I need to be baptized by you" (v. 3:14). The

Baptist, indeed, is aware of the great distance there is between him and Jesus. But Jesus has come precisely to bridge the gap between man and God: if he is completely on God's side, he is also completely on mankind's side, and reunites what had been separated. For this reason, he asks John to baptize him, so that all righteousness may be fulfilled (cf. v. 15). Namely, that the plan of God may be fulfilled, the plan which passes by way of obedience and solidarity with fragile and sinful mankind, the way of humility and of God's full closeness to his children. Because God is very close to us!

At the moment in which Jesus, baptized by John, comes out of the waters of the river Jordan, the voice of God the Father is heard from on high: "This is my beloved Son, with whom I am well pleased" (v. 17). At the same time the Holy Spirit, in the form of a dove, alights upon Jesus, who publicly begins his mission of salvation, a mission characterized by a manner: the way of a humble and gentle servant, armed only with the power of truth, as Isaiah had prophesied: "He will not cry or lift up his voice . . . a bruised reed he will not break, and a dimly burning wick he will not quench; he will faithfully bring forth justice" (cf. Is 42:2–3).

This is a humble and gentle servant. This is Jesus' way, as well as the manner of Christ's disciples' missionary work: to proclaim the Gospel with gentleness, but also firmness, without shouting, without reprimanding anyone, but gently and firmly, without arrogance or imposition. The true mission is never proselytism, but rather it's drawing people to Christ. But how? How is this attraction to Christ achieved? With one's own witness, starting from the unwavering union with him in prayer, in adoration, and in concrete works of charity, which is service to Jesus present in the least of his brothers and sisters. In imitation of Jesus, the good and merciful Shepherd, and moved by his grace, we are called to make our life a joyous testimony that illuminates the way, that brings hope and love.

This feast makes us rediscover the gift and the beauty of being a community of baptized, that is, of sinners—we all are sinners—saved by the grace of Christ, truly integrated, by the work of the Holy Spirit, in the filial relationship of Jesus with the Father, welcomed into the bosom of Mother Church, making possible a brotherhood that knows no barriers or borders.

May the Virgin Mary help all of us Christians to maintain an ever keen and grateful awareness of our own Baptism and to faithfully follow the path opened by this Sacrament of our rebirth. Ever with humility, gentleness, and firmness.

Readings from the Fathers of the Church

Saint Ambrose, The humility of Jesus

Jesus was man according to the flesh, but superior to man according to his capacity to act, and "as man he lowered himself" (Phil 2:7–8)—it is written—because God came to find and set free those who had been brought low. So he himself became lowly for us. His body is therefore not a body of death, precisely because it is the body of life, nor is his flesh a shadow of death, because it is the splendor of glory. Nor is there room for suffering in him, precisely because in his body there is the gift of consolation for all. He lowered himself to teach you humility. Listen to what he says: "Learn from me, who am meek and humble of heart!" (Mt 11:29). He lowered himself in order to exalt you: "Whoever humbles himself will be exalted" (Mt 23:12). But not all those who lower themselves will be exalted. There are many, in fact, who are lowered by sin to the point of their perdition. But the Lord lowered himself unto death, in order to be exalted from the gates of death.

This is the grace of Christ: take note of it, as also of the good that he has done for you!

Behold, the Lamb of God!
Second Sunday of Ordinary Time

+

John 1:29–34

29 The next day he saw Jesus coming toward him and said, "Behold, the Lamb of God, who takes away the sin of the world. 30 He is the one of whom I said, 'A man is coming after me who ranks ahead of me because he existed before me.' 31 I did not know him, but the reason why I came baptizing with water was that he might be made known to Israel."

At the center of today's Gospel reading (Jn 1:29–34) there is this message of John the Baptist: "Behold, the Lamb of God, who takes away the sin of the world!" (v. 29). It is a message accompanied by the gaze and the hand gesture that indicate him, Jesus.

Let us imagine the scene. We are on the bank of the river Jordan. John is baptizing; there are many people, men and women of various ages, who have come there, to the river, to receive Baptism from the hands of the man who reminded many of Elijah, the great prophet who nine centuries before had purified the Israelites of idolatry and led them back to the true faith in the God of the Covenant, the God of Abraham, Isaac, and Jacob.

John preaches that the Kingdom of Heaven is at hand, that the Messiah is about to reveal himself, and one must prepare, convert, and act with righteousness; and he begins to baptize in the river Jordan in order to give the people a tangible means of repentance (cf. Mt 3:1-6). These people came to repent of their sins, to make penance, to begin their life anew. He knows. John knows that the Messiah, the Lord's Consecrated One, is now nearby, and the sign to recognize him will be that the Holy Spirit will descend upon him. Indeed, he will bring the true Baptism, Baptism in the Holy Spirit (cf. Jn 1:33).

And thus, the moment arrives: Jesus appears on the riverbank, in the midst of the people, the sinners—like all of us. It is his first public act, the first thing he does when he leaves his home in Nazareth, at the age of thirty: he goes down into Judea, goes to the Jordan, and is baptized by John. We know what happens. We celebrated it last Sunday: the Holy Spirit descends upon Jesus in the form of a dove and the voice of the Father proclaims him the beloved Son (cf. Mt 3:16-17). It is the sign that John has been waiting for. It is he! Jesus is the Messiah. John is disconcerted, because he manifests himself in an unimaginable way: in the midst of sinners, baptized with them or, rather, for them. But the Spirit enlightens John and helps him understand that in this way God's justice is fulfilled, his plan of salvation is fulfilled: Jesus is the Messiah, the King of Israel; however, not with the power of this world but as the Lamb of God, who takes upon himself and takes away the sins of the world.

Thus, John points him out to the people and to his disciples. Because John had a large circle of disciples, who had chosen him as a spiritual guide, and some of them actually became the first disciples of Jesus. We know their names well: Simon, later called Peter, his brother Andrew, James and his brother John. All were fishermen, all Galileans, like Jesus.

Dear brothers and sisters, why have we focused so long on this scene? Because it is decisive! It is not an anecdote. It is a decisive historical fact! This scene is decisive for our faith; and it is also decisive for the Church's mission. The Church, in every time, is called to do what John the Baptist did: point Jesus out to the people, saying, "Behold, the Lamb of God, who takes away the sin of the world!" (Jn 1:29). He is the One Savior! He is the Lord, humble, in the midst of sinners, but it is he, he: there is no other powerful one who comes; no, no, it is he!

These are the words that we priests repeat each day, during the Mass, when we present to the people the bread and wine, which become the Body and Blood of Christ. This liturgical gesture represents the whole mission of the Church, which she does not proclaim herself. Woe, woe when the Church proclaims herself; she loses her bearings. She doesn't know where she is going! The Church proclaims Christ; she does not bring herself; she brings Christ. Because it is he and only he who saves his people from sin, frees them and guides them to land and to true freedom.

May the Virgin Mary, Mother of the Lamb of God, help us to believe in him and follow him.

Readings from the Fathers of the Church

Origen,
Jesus is the Lamb of God

At the feast of Passover it is written that it is *a lamb* that purifies the people (cf. Ex 12:3). [. . .] We say that this lamb is our Lord and Savior himself. John, the greatest of all the prophets, understood this and pointed him out, saying: "Behold the Lamb of God, behold him who takes away the sin of the world" (cf. Jn 1:29). [. . .] Of course, the Lord Jesus Christ is not called *lamb* because he changed and transformed into the form of a lamb! But nevertheless he is called *lamb*, because his will to do good—by which he brought God's favor back to men and leniency to sinners—was for the human race like the sacrifice of a spotless and innocent *lamb*, by which one has faith that the divine may reconcile the human.

So even if an angel, a heavenly power, a just man, or one of the holy prophets or apostles intercedes most ardently for the sins of men, in terms of reconciliation with God he could be considered as a *ram*, or a *calf*, or a *goat* offered in sacrifice to implore the purification of the people.

A Conversation
That Changes Hearts
Third Sunday of Ordinary Time

✛

Matthew 4:12–13; 17–23

12 When he heard that John had been arrested, he withdrew to Galilee. 13 He left Nazareth and went to live in Capernaum by the sea, in the region of Zebulun and Naphtali, . . . 17 Jesus began to preach and say, "Repent, for the kingdom of heaven is at hand." 18 As he was walking by the Sea of Galilee, he saw two brothers, Simon who is called Peter, and his brother Andrew, casting a net into the sea; they were fishermen. 19 He said to them, "Come after me, and I will make you fishers of men." 20 At once they left their nets and followed him. 21 He walked along from there and saw two other brothers, James, the son of Zebedee, and his brother John. They were in a boat, with their father Zebedee, mending their nets. He called them, 22 and immediately they left their boat and their father and followed him.

Today's Gospel passage (Mt 4:12–23) recounts the beginning of Jesus' preaching in Galilee. He leaves Nazareth, a village in the mountains, and settles in Capernaum, an important center on the lakeshore, inhabited largely by pagans, a crossroads between the Mediterranean and the Mesopotamian inland. This choice indicates that the beneficiaries of his preaching are not only his compatriots, but those who arrive in the cosmopolitan "Galilee of the Gentiles" (v. 15; cf. Is 8:23), for that's what it was called. Seen from the capital Jerusalem, that land is geographically peripheral and religiously impure because it was full of pagans, having mixed with those who did not belong to Israel. Great things were not expected from Galilee for the history of salvation. Instead, right from there—precisely from there—radiated that "light" on which we meditated in recent Sundays: the light of Christ. It radiated right from the periphery.

Jesus' message reiterates that of the Baptist, announcing the "kingdom of heaven" (v. 17). This Kingdom does not involve the establishment of a new political power, but the fulfillment of the Covenant between God and his people, which inaugurates a season of peace and justice. To secure this Covenant pact with God, each one is called to convert, transforming his or her way of thinking and living. This is important: converting is changing not only the way of life but also the way of thinking. It is a transformation of thought. It is a matter of changing not clothing, but habits!

What differentiates Jesus from John the Baptist is the way and manner. Jesus chooses to be an itinerant prophet. He doesn't stay and await people, but goes to encounter them. Jesus is always on the road! His first missionary appearances take place along the lake of Galilee, in contact with the multitude, in particular with the fishermen. There, Jesus does not only proclaim the coming of the Kingdom of God but seeks companions to join in his salvific mission. In this very place he meets two pairs of brothers: Simon and Andrew, James and John. He calls them, saying: "Follow me, and I will make you fishers of men" (v. 19). The call reaches them in the middle of their daily activity.

The Lord reveals himself to us not in an extraordinary or impressive way, but in the everyday circumstances of our life. There we must discover the Lord; and there he reveals himself, makes his love felt in our heart; and there—with this dialogue with him in the everyday circumstances of life—he changes our heart. The response of the four fishermen is immediate and willing: "Immediately they left their nets and followed him" (v. 20). We know, in fact, that they were disciples of the Baptist and that, thanks to his witness, they had already begun to believe in Jesus as the Messiah (cf. Jn 1:35–42).

We, today's Christians, have the joy of proclaiming and witnessing to our faith because there was that first announcement, because there were those humble and courageous men who responded generously to Jesus' call. On the shores of the lake, in an inconceivable land, the first community of disciples of Christ was born. May the knowledge of these beginnings give rise in us to the desire to bear Jesus' Word, love, and tenderness in every context, even the most difficult and resistant. To carry the Word to all the peripheries! All the spaces of human living are soil on which to cast the seeds of the Gospel, so they may bear the fruit of salvation.

May the Virgin Mary help us with her maternal intercession to respond joyfully to Jesus' call, and to place ourselves at the service of the Kingdom of God.

Readings from the Fathers of the Church

Saint Leo the Great,
God speaks in a gentle and friendly way

Dearly beloved, when the Lord Jesus Christ preached the Gospel of the Kingdom and throughout all of Galilee healed infirmities, the fame of his miracles spread throughout Syria, and in droves they came running to this heavenly physician from all over Judea. Since ignorant human faith is very slow to believe what it does not see and to hope in what it does not know, the divine wisdom had to attract it by means of bodily favors and visible miracles. [. . .] After caring for souls through the healing of bodies, he withdrew from the crowd surrounding him, went up onto a nearby mountain, and called the apostles to him. He filled their hearts with sublime teachings from the height of a mystical seat.

By choosing to preach from such a place, he wanted to indicate that it had been he himself who at one time had deigned to come down and converse with Moses. But there he had spoken with a rather tremendous justice, here instead he speaks with his more sacred clemency. [. . .]

The same one who had spoken to Moses now speaks with the apostles, and in the hearts of the disciples the rapid hand of the Word wrote the decrees of the New Testament. He was not surrounded, as in time past, by a mass of clouds, nor by terrible thunder and lightning, while the people stayed far from the mountain in terror. Now, instead, he spoke clearly for their ears and held a gentle dialogue with them, so that the gentleness of grace might remove the harshness of the law, and the spirit of adoption remove the terror of slavery.

Hope in God Never Disappoints

Feast of the Presentation of the Lord

✝

Luke 2:22–40

27 He came in the Spirit into the temple; and when the parents brought in the child Jesus to perform the custom of the law in regard to him, 28 he took him into his arms and blessed God, saying: 29 "Now, Master, you may let your servant go in peace, according to your word, 30 for my eyes have seen your salvation, 31 which you prepared in sight of all the peoples, 32 a light for revelation, to the Gentiles, and glory for your people Israel."

Today's liturgy presents us with Simeon, who, having come in the Spirit (Lk 2:27), takes the Child in his arms, and sings a song of blessing and praise. His heart rejoiced because God had come to dwell among his people; he felt his presence in the flesh.

Simeon's canticle is the hymn of the believer, who at the end of his days can exclaim: "Hope does not disappoint" (Rom 5:5). God never deceives us. Simeon and Anna, in their old age, were capable of a new fruitfulness, and they testify to this in song. Life is worth living in hope, because the Lord keeps his promise.

We have inherited this hymn of hope from our elders. They made us part of this process. In their faces, in their lives, in their daily sacrifice we are able to see how this praise was embodied. We are heirs to the dreams of our elders, heirs of their hope.

We do well to take up the dreams of our elders, so that we can prophesy in our day and once more encounter what originally set our hearts afire. Dreams and prophecies together—the remembrance of how our elders, our fathers and mothers, dreamed—and the courage prophetically to carry on those dreams.

This attitude will make our consecrated life more fruitful, but most important, it will protect us from a temptation that can make our consecrated life barren: the temptation of survival, an evil that can gradually take root within us and within our communities. The mentality of survival makes us reactionaries, fearful, slowly and silently shutting ourselves up in our houses and in our own preconceived notions. It makes us look back, to the glory days—days that are past. And rather than rekindling the prophetic creativity born of our founders' dreams, it looks for shortcuts in order to evade the challenges knocking on our doors today. A survival mentality robs our charisms of power, because it leads us to "domesticate" them, to make them "user-friendly," robbing them of their original creative force. It makes us want to protect spaces, buildings, and structures, rather than to encourage new initiatives. The temptation of survival makes us forget grace. It turns us into professionals of the sacred, but not fathers and mothers, brothers and sisters of that hope to which we are called to bear prophetic witness. An environment of survival withers the hearts of our elderly, taking away their ability to dream. In this way, it cripples the prophecy that our young are called to proclaim and work to achieve. In a word, the temptation of survival turns what the Lord presents as an opportunity for mission into something dangerous, threatening, potentially disastrous.

Surely, the song of Simeon and Anna was not the fruit of self-absorption or an analysis and review of their personal situation. It did not ring out because they were caught up in themselves and were worried that something bad might happen to them. Their song was born of hope, the hope that sustained them in their old age. That hope was rewarded when they encountered Jesus. When Mary let Simeon take the Son of the Promise into his arms, the old man began to sing—celebrating a true "liturgy." He sang his dreams.

Whenever Mary puts Jesus in the midst of his people, they encounter joy. For this alone will bring back our joy and hope, this alone will save us from living in a survival mentality. Only this will make our lives fruitful and keep our hearts alive: putting Jesus where he belongs, in the midst of his people.

To put ourselves with Jesus in the midst of his people, what fruitfulness! And not as religious "activists," but as men and women who are constantly forgiven, men and women anointed in Baptism and sent to share that anointing and the consolation of God with everyone.

To put ourselves with Jesus in the midst of his people

keeps our hearts alive! For this reason, "we sense the challenge of finding and sharing a 'mystique' of living together, of mingling and encountering, of embracing and supporting one another, of stepping into this flood tide which, while chaotic, can [with the Lord] become a genuine experience of fraternity, a caravan of solidarity, a sacred pilgrimage. . . . If we were able to take this route, it would be so good, so soothing, so liberating and hope-filled! To go out of ourselves and to join others" (*Evangelii Gaudium*, 87) is not only good for us. It also turns our lives and hopes into a hymn of praise. But we will only be able to do this if we take up the dreams of our elders and turn them into prophecy.

> Let us accompany Jesus as he goes forth to meet his people, to be in the midst of his people. Let us go forth, not with the complaining or anxiety of those who have forgotten how to prophesy because they failed to take up the dreams of their elders, but with serenity and songs of praise. Not with apprehension, but with the patience of those who trust in the Spirit, the Lord of dreams and prophecy. In this way, let us share what is truly our own: the hymn that is born of hope.

Readings from the Fathers of the Church

Saint Sophronius,
The light that enlightens every man

This is our mystery: "The light has come into the world" (Jn 3:19). And man, being in darkness, it has enlightened him, because "the dawn from on high has come to visit us" (Lk 1:78) and has enlightened those who are in darkness. So let us all go running together; let us go to meet God, lest in hesitating to do so we be accused of ingratitude or great contempt toward him and hear him say quite justly that which the Jews, truly enveloped in darkness and devoid of light, were the first to hear him say: "The light has come into the world, but men preferred the darkness to the light, because their works were evil" (Jn 3:19). [. . .] So the true light comes that enlightens every man who comes into the world (cf. Jn 1:9). Brothers, let us all be enlightened; brothers, let us all shine. Let none of us remain uninitiated into the light; let none of us remain infected with the darkness. Come, let us all go forth shining. All together, enlightened, let us go to meet and welcome with the aged Simeon the shining and eternal light and, exulting with him in the Spirit, let us sing a hymn of thanksgiving to the Father and creator of the light, who has sent the true light, who has driven the darkness from us and made us all radiant. We too have seen in him the salvation of God prepared before all the people and brought forth for the glory of the new Israel that we are. And indeed we were set free right away from the dark old sin, just as Simeon, seeing Christ, was set free from this life.

Faith Gives "Flavor" to Life

Fifth Sunday of Ordinary Time

✝

Matthew 5:13–16

13 "You are the salt of the earth. But if salt loses its taste, with what can it be seasoned? It is no longer good for anything but to be thrown out and trampled underfoot. 14 You are the light of the world. A city set on a mountain cannot be hidden. 15 Nor do they light a lamp and then put it under a bushel basket; it is set on a lampstand, where it gives light to all in the house. 16 Just so, your light must shine before others, that they may see your good deeds and glorify your heavenly Father."

These Sundays the liturgy offers us the so-called Sermon on the Mount, in the Gospel of Matthew. After presenting the Beatitudes last Sunday, today [Matthew] emphasizes Jesus' words describing his disciples' mission in the world (Mt 5:13–16). He uses the metaphors of salt and light, and his words are directed to the disciples of every age, therefore also to us.

Jesus invites us to be a reflection of his light, by witnessing with good works. He says: "Your light must shine before others, that they may see your good deeds and glorify your heavenly Father" (v. 16). These words emphasize that we are recognizable as true disciples of the One who is the Light of the World, not in words, but by our works. Indeed, it is above all our behavior that—good or bad—leaves a mark on others. Therefore, we have a duty and a responsibility toward the gift received: the light of the faith, which is in us through Christ and the action of the Holy Spirit; and we must not withhold it as if it were our property. Instead, we are called to make it shine throughout the world, to offer it to others through good works. How much the world needs the light of the Gospel, which transforms, heals, and guarantees salvation to those who receive it! We must convey this light through our good works.

The light of our faith, in giving of oneself, does not fade but strengthens. However, it can weaken if we do not nourish it with love and with charitable works. In this way, the image of light complements that of salt. The Gospel passage, in fact, tells us that, as disciples of Christ, we are also "the salt of the earth" (v. 13). Salt is an ingredient which, while it gives flavor, keeps food from turning and spoiling—in Jesus' time there were no refrigerators! Thus, Christians' mission in society is that of giving "flavor" to life with the faith and the love that Christ has given us, and at the same time keeping away the contaminating seeds of selfishness, envy, slander, and so on. These seeds degrade the fabric of our communities, which should instead shine as places of welcome, solidarity, and reconciliation. To fulfill this mission, it is essential that we first free ourselves from the corruptive degeneration of worldly influences contrary to Christ and to the Gospel. And this purification never ends. It must be done continuously; it must be done every day!

Again, salt becomes salt once it is given. This is another attitude for the Christian to embody: to give oneself to others, to flavor all things with the message of the Gospel. Don't keep it all for yourself. Salt is not for the Christian to hold on to; it is to be given away. The Christian is to give it away, in order for salt to become salt.

Each one of us is called to be light and salt, in the environment of our daily life, persevering in the task of regenerating the human reality in the spirit of the Gospel and in the perspective of the Kingdom of God.

May there always be the helpful protection of Mary Most Holy, first disciple of Jesus and model for believers who live their vocation and mission each day in history. May our Mother help us to let ourselves always be purified and enlightened by the Lord, so as to become, in our turn, "salt of the earth" and "light of the world."

Readings from the Fathers of the Church

Saint Chromatius of Aquileia,
What does it mean to be salt of the earth?

The Lord calls his apostles salt of the earth. Let us see what the Lord means to say about his apostles with the comparison suggested by this word. [. . .] They, in fact, have become the salt of our earth, because through them we have received the word of wisdom and by heavenly birth have been transformed into a spiritual nature. [. . .]

Therefore, just as salt acting on any kind of meat prevents rot, removes odors, cleanses filth, keeps maggots from hatching, so also the heavenly grace that has been given through the apostles acts in us by a similar process. It takes away, in fact, the rot of the concupiscence of the flesh, cleanses the filth of sins, removes the odor of a bad life, keeps the maggots of our faults from hatching—meaning the lustful and deadly pleasures that arise from the body—preserving our body even from that immortal worm which with an incessant pain torments sinners, of which it is written: "Their worm will not die, and their fire will not be extinguished" (Is 66:24). And just as salt is applied on the outside but acts on the inside through the properties of its nature, so also heavenly grace penetrates both the outside and inside of man and keeps the whole of him intact from sin and unspoiled. [. . .]

So, the Lord is not wrong when he calls his apostles salt of the earth, because he filled them with himself and with heavenly wisdom. Thus, he affirmed that they were salt of the earth, as also the light of the world.

Being Christians
Not "of Façade," but of Substance
Sixth Sunday of Ordinary Time

☩

Matthew 5:17–37

17 "Do not think that I have come to abolish the law or the prophets. I have come not to abolish but to fulfill. . . . 20 I tell you, unless your righteousness surpasses that of the scribes and Pharisees, you will not enter into the kingdom of heaven. 21 You have heard that it was said to your ancestors, 'You shall not kill; and whoever kills will be liable to judgment.' 22 But I say to you, whoever is angry with his brother will be liable to judgment, and whoever says to his brother, 'Raqa,' will be answerable to the Sanhedrin, and whoever says, 'You fool,' will be liable to fiery Gehenna. . . . 27 You have heard that it was said, 'You shall not commit adultery.' 28 But I say to you, everyone who looks at a woman with lust has already committed adultery with her in her heart. . . . 33 Again you have heard that it was said to your ancestors, 'Do not take a false oath, but make good to the Lord all that you vow.' 34 But I say to you, do not swear at all; . . . 37 Let your 'Yes' mean 'Yes,' and your 'No' mean 'No.' Anything more is from the evil one."

Today's liturgy presents us with another passage of the Sermon on the Mount, which we find in the Gospel of Saint Matthew (5:17–37). In this passage, Jesus wants to help his listeners to reread the Mosaic law. What had been said in the ancient Covenant was true, but that was not all: Jesus came to bring to fulfillment and to promulgate in a definitive way the Law of God, up to the last iota (cf. v. 18). He manifests its original aims and fulfills its authentic aspects, and he does all this through his preaching and, even more, with the offering of himself on the Cross. In this way, Jesus teaches how to fully carry out God's will, and he uses these words: with a "righteousness" that "exceeds" that of the scribes and the Pharisees (cf. v. 20). A righteousness enlivened by love, charity, mercy, and hence capable of fulfilling the substance of the commandments, avoiding the risk of formalism. Formalism: this I can, this I cannot; up to this point I can, up to this point I cannot. . . . No: more, more.

In particular, in today's Gospel, Jesus examines three aspects: three commandments [that focus on] murder, adultery, and swearing.

With regard to the commandment "you shall not kill," he states that it is violated not only by murder in effect, but also by those behaviors that offend the dignity of the human person, including insulting words (cf. v. 22). Of course, these insulting words do not have the same gravity and culpability as killing, but they are set along the same line, because they are the pretext to it, and they reveal the same malevolence. Jesus invites us not to establish a ranking of offenses, but to consider all of them damaging, inasmuch as they are driven by the intent to do harm to one's neighbor. Jesus gives an example. Insulting: we are accustomed to insulting; it is like saying "good morning." And that is on the same line as killing. One who insults his brother in his heart kills his brother. Please do not insult! We do not gain anything by it. . . .

Another fulfillment is generated by the matrimonial law. Adultery was considered a violation of the man's property right over the woman. Instead, Jesus goes to the root of the evil. As one comes to killing through injuries, offenses, and insults, in this way one reaches adultery through covetous intentions in regard to a woman other than one's own wife. Adultery, like theft, corruption, and all the other sins, is first conceived in the depth of our being and, once the wrong choice is made in the heart, it is carried out in concrete behavior. Jesus says: one who looks with a covetous spirit at a woman who is not his own is an adulterer in his heart, has set off on the path toward adultery. Let us think a little bit about this: about the wicked thoughts that go along this line.

Jesus then tells his disciples not to swear, as swearing is a sign of the insecurity and duplicity with which human relationships unfold. God's authority is exploited so as to guarantee our human narrative. Instead, we are called to establish among ourselves, in our families and in our communities, a climate of clarity and mutual trust, so that we can be considered sincere without resorting to greater tactics in order to be believed. Mistrust and mutual suspicion always threaten peace!

May the Virgin Mary, a woman of listening and joyful obedience, help us to draw ever closer to the Gospel, to be
Christians not "of façade," but of substance! This is possible with the grace of the Holy Spirit, who allows us to do
everything with love, and thus to wholly fulfill the will of
God.

Readings from the Fathers of the Church

Saint Dorotheus,
Let us bear insults if we know ourselves to be sinners

Let us consider, brothers, why it is that sometimes we hear a
hurtful comment and let it go without getting upset, as if we
had not even heard it, while other times we need only hear it
and right away we get upset. What is the reason for this difference? [. . .] First of all, it happens that we have just finished
praying or performing a nice meditation and we find ourselves,
so to speak, in good shape, and then we bear with our brother
and move on without getting upset. Other times it happens
that we have an attachment to someone, and for this reason
we bear without distressing ourselves that which comes from
him.

I want to recount for you an episode that will amaze you.
In the cenobium [monastery of life in community], before I
went away, there was a brother whom I never saw upset or
distressed with anyone; and yet I saw that many brothers mistreated him and pushed him around in various ways. One day
I took him aside [. . .] and invited him to tell me what thought
he always had in his heart, whether he was mistreated or dealt

with rudely, seeing that he showed such patience. He replied frankly to me and said: "All I have to do is look out for these injustices and accept them the way dogs do." When I heard this, I lowered my eyes and said to myself: "This brother has found the way!" And after making the sign of the Cross, I went away praying to God that he protect both me and him.

A Christian "Revolution"

Seventh Sunday of Ordinary Time

+

Matthew 5:38–48

43 "You have heard that it was said, 'You shall love your neighbor and hate your enemy.' 44 But I say to you, love your enemies, and pray for those who persecute you, 45 that you may be children of your heavenly Father, for he makes his sun rise on the bad and the good, and causes rain to fall on the just and the unjust. 46 For if you love those who love you, what recompense will you have? Do not the tax collectors do the same? 47 And if you greet your brothers only, what is unusual about that? Do not the pagans do the same? 48 So be perfect, just as your heavenly Father is perfect."

In this Sunday's Gospel (Mt 5:38–48)—one of the passages that best illustrates Christian "revolution"—Jesus shows us the way of true justice through the law of love, which is greater than the law of retaliation, "an eye for an eye and a tooth for a tooth." This ancient law imposed the infliction on wrongdoers of a punishment equivalent to the damage they caused: death for those who killed, amputation for those who injured, and so on. Jesus does not ask his disciples to abide evil, but asks them to react; however, not with another evil action, but with good. This is the only way to break the chain of evil: one evil leads to another, which leads to another evil. . . . This chain of evil is broken, and things truly begin to change. Evil is, in fact, a "void," a void of good. It is not possible to fill a void, except with "fullness," that is, good. Revenge never leads to conflict resolution. "You did this to me, I will do it back to you": this never resolves conflict, nor is it even Christian.

According to Jesus, the rejection of violence can also involve the sacrifice of a legitimate right. He gives a few examples of this: turn the other cheek, give up your coat or money, accept other sacrifices (v. 39–42). But such sacrifice does not mean that the demands of justice should be ignored or contradicted. No, on the contrary, Christian love, which manifests itself in a special way in mercy, is an achievement superior to justice. What Jesus wants to teach us is the clear distinction that we must make between justice and revenge. Distinguishing between justice and revenge: revenge is never just. We are permitted to ask for justice. It is our duty to exercise justice. We are, however, not permitted to avenge ourselves or in any way foment revenge, as it is an expression of hatred and violence. Jesus teaches us this not only to fulfill the law but also to heal our hearts.

Jesus wishes to propose not a new system of civil law but rather the commandment to love thy neighbor, which also includes loving enemies: "Love your enemies and pray for those who persecute you" (v. 44). And this is not easy. These words should be seen not as an approval of evil carried out by an enemy but as an invitation to a loftier perspective, a magnanimous perspective, similar to that of the Heavenly Father, who, Jesus says, "makes his sun rise on the bad and the good, and causes rain to fall on the just and the unjust" (v. 45). An enemy, in fact, is also a human being, created as such in God's image, despite the fact that, in the present, that image may be tarnished by shameful behavior.

When we speak of "enemies," we should not think about people who are different or far removed from us; let us also talk about ourselves, as we may come into conflict with our neighbor, at times with our relatives. How many hostilities exist within families—how many! Let us think about this. Enemies are also those who speak ill of us, who defame us and do us harm. It is not easy to digest this. We are called to respond to each of them with good, which also has strategies inspired by love.

May the Lord give us the grace to pray for our enemies, for those who persecute us. These prayers will heal us, because prayer is powerful and makes us more aware that we are children of the Father.

May the Virgin Mary help us follow Jesus on this demanding path, which truly exalts human dignity and lets us live as children of our Father who art in heaven. May she help us to exercise patience, dialogue, forgiveness, and to be artisans of communion, artisans of fraternity in our daily life, and above all in our families.

Readings from the Fathers of the Church

Saint Ambrose,
Jesus forgave his own executioners

If returning love is common to all, even to sinners, he who professes a higher faith must also pay more fruitful attention to virtue, for the sake of loving even those who do not love him. [. . .] The Lord Jesus, going beyond the words inspired by the Law and the highest summits of philosophy, wanted the obligation of mercy to be extended also to those who wrong us. [. . .] All of this the Lord said and did. He, when he was insulted did not respond with insults (cf. 1 Pt 2:23), when he was struck he did not return the blows, when he was stripped he put up no resistance, when he was crucified he pleaded for the forgiveness of his own executioners, saying: "Father, forgive them, because they do not know what they are doing" (Lk 23:34). He held blameless of all fault those who had blamed him. For him they were preparing the Cross, he in exchange was giving salvation and love. And yet, since even the effort for virtue grows slack if it finds no recompense, he gave us the example and promised us the prize of Heaven, giving assurance that his imitators would become children of God (cf. 1 Jn 3:1). [. . .]

But how great is this merciful recompense, through which we are granted the right to become children of God! Follow mercy, then, in order to merit grace. The kindness of God has no limits: he makes it rain upon the ungrateful (cf. Mt 5:45).

Free Yourself from the Power of Appearance

Ash Wednesday

+

Matthew 6:1–6, 17–18

1 "[But] take care not to perform righteous deeds in order that people may see them; otherwise, you will have no recompense from your heavenly Father. . . . 3 But when you give alms, do not let your left hand know what your right is doing, 4 so that your almsgiving may be secret. And your Father who sees in secret will repay you. . . . 6 But when you pray, go to your inner room, close the door, and pray to your Father in secret. And your Father who sees in secret will repay you. . . . 17 But when you fast, anoint your head and wash your face, 18 so that you may not appear to others to be fasting, except to your Father who is hidden. And your Father who sees what is hidden will repay you."

In today's Gospel, Jesus speaks of almsgiving, prayer, and fasting. These are the three pillars of Christian piety, which Lent encourages us toward. These pillars are not built on appearances, for the value of life depends not on others' approval or on success, but on the content of our interior lives. The Lord mentions another class of hypocrites: those concerned with the sacred—that is, those who pray, fast, and give alms. When hypocrisy reaches that point, it touches on sin against the Holy Spirit. This hypocrisy knows nothing of beauty, nor love, nor truth; rather, it is small, cowardly. And none of us are immune from practicing such hypocrisy.

The first pillar of Lent is almsgiving. Jesus warns us about this risk of the bribe: we take away from our penance, from our acts of prayer, of fasting, of almsgiving; we accept a "bribe": the bribe of vanity, of making ourselves seen. That is not authenticity, but hypocrisy. When Jesus says, "When you pray, do so in secret; when you give alms, sound no trumpet; when you fast, do not look dismal," it is the same as if he were to say, "Please, when you do a good deed, do not take the bribe of this good deed, it is only for the Father."

The second pillar is prayer. Prayer is the strength of the Christian and of every person who believes. In the weakness and frailty of our lives, we can turn to God with the confidence of children and enter into communion with him. In the face of so many wounds that hurt us and could harden our hearts, we are called to dive into the sea of prayer, which is the sea of God's boundless love, to taste his tenderness. Lent is a time of prayer, of more intense prayer, more prolonged, more assiduous, more able to take on the needs of the brethren—intercessory prayer, to intercede before God for the many situations of poverty and suffering.

The third pillar of the Lenten journey is fasting. We must be careful not to practice a formal fast, or one which in truth "satisfies" us because it makes us feel good about ourselves. Fasting makes sense if it questions our security, and if it also leads to some benefit for others, if it helps us to cultivate the style of the Good Samaritan, who bends down to his brother in need and takes care of him. Fasting involves choosing a sober lifestyle, a way of life that does not waste, a way of life that does not "throw away." Fasting helps us to attune our hearts to the essential and to sharing. It is a sign of awareness and responsibility in the face of injustice, abuse, especially to the poor and the little ones, and it is a sign of the trust we place in God and in his providence.

We ask the Lord to save us from all hypocrisy and give us the grace of love, of generosity, of magnanimity, of joy.

Readings from the Fathers of the Church

Barnabas, *The way of light*

This, therefore, is the way of light. [. . .] You shall love him who created you, you shall fear him who formed you, you shall glorify him who freed you from death. You shall be simple of heart and rich in spirit, and you shall not join those who walk the path of death. You shall hate all that which does not please God and all hypocrisy, and you shall not abandon the precepts of the Lord. You shall not boast, but shall instead be humble in everything without seeking glory for yourself. You shall not harbor evil intentions toward your neighbor, and you shall not allow arrogance into your soul. You shall commit no fornication, adultery, or corruption of children. Do not let out the Word of God among the depraved. Have no consideration of persons in reprimanding the fallen. You shall be meek, at peace, and shall fear the words that you have heard. You shall have no rancor against your brother. Do not wonder whether this or that will happen or not. You shall not take the name of the Lord in vain. You shall love your neighbor more than your soul. You shall not kill a child whether still in the womb or already born. Do not withhold your hand from your son or daughter, but from childhood you shall teach them the fear of God. Do not covet your neighbor's goods, or be greedy. Do not attach your soul to the arrogant, but rather be found with the humble and the just. Accept what happens to you as a good, knowing that nothing takes place apart from God.

Answer Only with the Word of God

First Sunday of Lent

+

Matthew 4:1–11

3 The tempter approached and said to him, "If you are the Son of God, command that these stones become loaves of bread." 4 He said in reply, "It is written: 'One does not live by bread alone, but by every word that comes forth from the mouth of God.'" . . . 8 Then the devil took him up to a very high mountain, and showed him all the kingdoms of the world in their magnificence, 9 and he said to him, "All these I shall give to you, if you will prostrate yourself and worship me." 10 At this, Jesus said to him, "Get away, Satan! It is written: 'The Lord, your God, shall you worship and him alone shall you serve.'" 11 Then the devil left him and, behold, angels came and ministered to him.

I n this First Sunday of Lent, the Gospel introduces us to the journey toward Easter, revealing Jesus as he remains in the desert for forty days, subjected to the temptations of the devil (Mt 4:1–11). This episode takes place at a precise moment in Jesus' life: immediately after his Baptism in the river Jordan and prior to his public ministry. He has just received the solemn investiture: the Spirit of God has descended upon him, the heavenly Father has declared him "my beloved Son" (v. 17). Jesus is now ready to begin his mission; and as this mission has a declared enemy, namely, Satan, he confronts him straightaway, "up close." The devil plays precisely on the title "Son of God" in order to deter Jesus from the fulfillment of his mission—"If you are the Son of God" (4:3, 6)—and proposes that he perform miraculous acts—be a "magician"—such as transforming stones into bread to satiate his hunger, and throwing himself down from the temple wall to be saved by the angels. These two temptations are followed by the third: to worship him, the devil, to have dominion over the world (cf. v. 9).

Through this threefold temptation, Satan wants to divert Jesus from the way of obedience and humiliation—because he knows that in this way, on this path, evil will be conquered—and to lead him down the false shortcut to success and glory. But the devil's poisonous arrows are "blocked" by Jesus with the shield of God's Word (vv. 4, 10), which expresses the will of the Father. Jesus does not speak a word of his own: he responds only with the Word of God. Thus, the Son, filled with the power of the Holy Spirit, comes out of the desert victorious.

During the forty days of Lent, as Christians we are invited to follow in Jesus' footsteps and face the spiritual battle with the Evil One with the strength of the Word of God. Not with our words: they are worthless. The Word of God: this has the strength to defeat Satan. For this reason, it is important to be familiar with the Bible: read it often, meditate on it, assimilate it. The Bible contains the Word of God, which is always timely and effective. Someone has asked: What would happen were we to treat the Bible as we treat our mobile phone? Were we to always carry it with us, or at least a small, pocket-sized Gospel, what would happen? Were we to turn back when we forget it—you forget your mobile phone: "Oh! I don't have it, I'm going back to look for it"; were we to open it several times a day; were we to read God's messages contained in the Bible as we read telephone messages, what would happen? Clearly the comparison is paradoxical, but it calls for reflection. Indeed, if we had God's Word always in our heart, no temptation could separate us from God, and no obstacle could divert us from the path of good; we would know how to defeat the daily temptations of the evil that is within us and outside us; we would be more capable of living a life renewed according to the Spirit, welcoming and loving our brothers and sisters, especially the weakest and neediest, and also our enemies.

May the Virgin Mary, perfect icon of obedience to God and of unconditional trust in his will, sustain us on the Lenten journey, that we may set ourselves to listen docilely to the Word of God in order to achieve a true conversion of heart.

Readings from the Fathers of the Church

Saint Augustine,
It is the Spirit who speaks in you

No one should count on his own wisdom when he speaks; no one should trust in his own strength when he suffers temptation. In fact, for our speech to be upright and prudent, our wisdom must come from God; and for us to bear evils with fortitude, our patience must also come from him.

Consider the Lord Jesus Christ who, according to the Gospel, alerts his disciples; consider the King of the martyrs who provides his ranks with the weapons of the spirit, anticipates wars, administers resources, promises payment. After telling his disciples, "in this world you will be in tribulations," in order to reassure their terrified hearts he immediately went on to say: "but have confidence, because I have defeated the world" (cf. Jn 16:33). [. . .]

"In this world," the Lord says, "you will be in tribulations," but in such a way that if the tribulation brings anxiety, it may not become oppressive, and if it attacks, it may not conquer. Against the soldiers of Christ the world unsheathes a two-edged sword. [. . .] It flatters them, in fact, to lead them into error, and it terrorizes them to break down their resistance. Let us not be carried away by the impulse to preserve ourselves, let us not be frightened by the cruelty that is brought against us, and the world is defeated. And, since Christ stands guard at both of these ways of attack, there is no defeat for the Christian. [. . .]

Therefore, to those he was deploying for combat of this sort, he addressed these words in the Gospel: "Do not worry about how to talk or what to say. In fact, it is not you who speak, but the Spirit of your Father who speaks in you" (cf. Mt 10:19–20).

The Cross,
the Door of the Resurrection

Second Sunday of Lent

✝

Matthew 17:1–9

1 After six days Jesus took Peter, James, and John his brother, and led them up a high mountain by themselves. 2 And he was transfigured before them; his face shone like the sun and his clothes became white as light. . . . 5 While he was still speaking, behold, a bright cloud cast a shadow over them, then from the cloud came a voice that said, "This is my beloved Son, with whom I am well pleased; listen to him." 6 When the disciples heard this, they fell prostrate and were very much afraid. 7 But Jesus came and touched them, saying, "Rise, and do not be afraid." 8 And when the disciples raised their eyes, they saw no one else but Jesus alone. 9 As they were coming down from the mountain, Jesus charged them, "Do not tell the vision to anyone until the Son of Man has been raised from the dead."

The Gospel of this Second Sunday of Lent presents the narrative of the Transfiguration of Jesus. The "brightness" which characterizes this extraordinary event symbolizes its purpose: to enlighten the minds and hearts of the disciples so that they may clearly understand who their Teacher is. It is a flash of light which suddenly opens onto the mystery of Jesus and illuminates his whole person and his whole story.

By now decisively headed toward Jerusalem, where he will be sentenced to death by crucifixion, Jesus wanted to prepare his own for this scandal—the scandal of the Cross—this scandal which is too intense for their faith, and, at the same time, to foretell his Resurrection by manifesting himself as *the Messiah, the Son of God*. Jesus was preparing them for that sad and very painful moment. In fact, Jesus was already revealing himself as a Messiah different from their expectations, from how they imagined the Messiah, how the Messiah would be: not a powerful and glorious king, but a humble and unarmed servant; not a lord of great wealth, a sign of blessing, but a poor man with nowhere to rest his head; not a patriarch with many descendants, but a celibate man without home or nest. It is truly an overturned revelation of God, and the most bewildering sign of this scandalous overturning is the Cross. But it is through the Cross that Jesus will reach the glorious Resurrection, which will be definitive, not like this Transfiguration, which lasted a moment, an instant.

Transfigured on Mount Tabor, Jesus wanted to show his disciples his glory, not for them to circumvent the Cross, but to show *where the Cross leads*. Those who die with Jesus shall rise again with Jesus. The Cross is the door to Resurrection. Whoever struggles alongside him will triumph with him. This is the message of hope contained in Jesus' Cross, urging us to be strong in our existence. The Christian Cross is not the furnishings of a house or adornments to wear. Rather, the Christian Cross is a call to the love with which Jesus sacrificed himself to save humanity from evil and sin. In this Lenten season, we contemplate with devotion the image of the Crucifix, Jesus on the Cross: this is the symbol of Christian faith, the emblem of Jesus, who died and rose for us. Let us ensure that the Cross marks the stages of our Lenten journey in order to understand ever better the seriousness of sin and the value of the sacrifice by which the Savior has saved us all.

During the Transfiguration, the voice of the Father resounds, proclaiming Jesus to be his most beloved Son, saying, "Listen to him" (Mt 17:5). This word is important! Our Father said this to these apostles, and says it to us as well: "Listen to Jesus, because he is my beloved Son." This week let us keep this word in our minds and in our hearts: "Listen to Jesus!" The pope is not saying this. God the Father says it to everyone: to me, to you, to everyone, all people! It is like an aid for going forward on the path of Lent. "Listen to Jesus!"

From the event of the Transfiguration I would like to take two significant elements that can be summed up in two words: *ascent* and *descent*. We all need to go apart, to ascend the mountain in a space of silence, to find ourselves and better perceive the voice of the Lord. This we do in prayer. But we cannot stay there! Encounter with God in prayer inspires us anew to "descend the mountain" and return to the plain, where we meet many brothers and sisters weighed down by fatigue, sickness, injustice, ignorance, poverty both material and spiritual. To these brothers and sisters in difficulty, we are called to bear the fruit of that experience with God, by sharing the grace we have received. And this is curious. When we hear the Word of Jesus, when we listen to the Word of Jesus and carry it in our heart, this Word grows. Do you know how it grows? By giving it to the other! The Word of Christ grows in us when we proclaim it, when we give it to others! And this is what Christian life is. It is a mission for the whole Church, for all the baptized, for us all: listen to Jesus and offer him to others. Do not forget: this week, listen to Jesus!

The Blessed Virgin was able to contemplate the glory of Jesus hidden in his humanness. May she help us stay with him in silent prayer, to allow ourselves to be enlightened by his presence, so as to bring a reflection of his glory to our hearts through the darkest nights.

Readings from the Fathers of the Church

Saint Justin, *The mystery of the Cross*

On this point they accuse us of madness, since we affirm that we assign the second place—right after the immutable, eternal God and creator of all things—to a crucified man, but they do not know the mystery that this contains and on which we urge you to reflect under our guidance. [. . .]

Nowhere did any of those who were believed to be sons of Zeus imitate death on a cross; this they did not understand, since as we have already shown all of the statements concerning this event were made in a symbolic manner. And this, as the prophet foretold, is the greatest symbol of his strength and his power, as is shown by the things that happen right before our eyes. Think about all of the things that there are in the universe, if they could ever endure without this form [of the Cross] or be unified. For the sea cannot be traversed unless the sign of victory, which is called a sail, remains fast in the ship. Without it the earth is not plowed; similarly diggers cannot do their work, nor can craftsmen, if they do not have tools according to this design.

Man's form does not distinguish itself in any other way from that of the unreasoning beasts, if not by standing upright with the hands reaching side to side, and by having on his face that which, jutting out beneath the forehead, is called a nose, which brings the breath of life and depicts none other than the form of the cross.

The prophet said it like this: "The breath of our face is Christ the Lord" (cf. Lam 4:20).

The Thirsty Soul Before Jesus
Third Sunday of Lent

✝

John 4:5–42

6 Jesus, tired from his journey, sat down there at the well. It was about noon. 7 A woman of Samaria came to draw water. Jesus said to her, "Give me a drink." 8 His disciples had gone into the town to buy food. 9 The Samaritan woman said to him, "How can you, a Jew, ask me, a Samaritan woman, for a drink?" . . . 10 Jesus answered and said to her, "If you knew the gift of God and who is saying to you, 'Give me a drink,' you would have asked him and he would have given you living water." . . . 13 Jesus answered and said to her, "Everyone who drinks this water will be thirsty again; 14 but whoever drinks the water I shall give will never thirst; the water I shall give will become in him a spring of water welling up to eternal life." 15 The woman said to him, "Sir, give me this water, so that I may not be thirsty or have to keep coming here to draw water." . . . 25 The woman said to him, "I know that the Messiah is coming, the one called the Anointed; when he comes, he will tell us everything." 26 Jesus said to her, "I am he, the one who is speaking with you."

The Gospel for this Third Sunday of Lent presents Jesus' dialogue with the Samaritan woman. While the disciples go into the village to buy food, Jesus stays near a well and asks a woman for a drink; she had come there to draw water. Jesus' thirst was not so much for water but for the encounter with a parched soul. Jesus needed to encounter the Samaritan woman in order to open her heart: he asks for a drink so as to bring to light her own thirst.

"How can you, a Jew, ask me, a Samaritan woman, for a drink?"

Jesus responded, "If you knew the gift of God and who is saying to you, 'Give me a drink,' you would have asked him and he would have given you living water" (Jn 4:9–10).

The woman is moved by this encounter. She asks Jesus several profound questions that we all carry within but often ignore. We too have many questions to ask, but we don't have the courage to ask Jesus! Lent, dear brothers and sisters, is the opportune time to look within ourselves, to understand our truest spiritual needs, and to ask the Lord's help in prayer. The example of the Samaritan woman invites us to exclaim: "Sir, give me this water, so that I may not be thirsty or have to keep coming here to draw water." Going to the well to draw water is burdensome and tedious; it would be lovely to have a gushing spring available! But Jesus speaks of a different water. When the woman realizes that the man she is speaking with is a prophet, she confides in him about her own life and asks him religious questions. Her thirst for affection and a full life had not been satisfied by the five husbands she had had, but instead, she had experienced disappointment and deceit. Thus, the woman was struck by the great respect Jesus had for her. And when he actually spoke to her of true faith as the relationship with God the Father "in spirit and truth," she realized that this man could be the Messiah. Then Jesus does something extremely rare—he confirms it: "I am he, the one who is speaking with you" (v. 26). He proclaims that he is the Messiah to a woman who led such a disordered life.

Dear brothers and sisters, the water that gives eternal life was poured into our hearts on the day of our Baptism; then God transformed and filled us with his grace. But we may have forgotten this great gift we received, or reduced it to a merely official statistic. Perhaps we seek "wells" whose water does not quench our thirst. When we forget the true water, we go in search of wells that do not have clean water. Thus, this Gospel passage actually concerns us! Not just the Samaritan woman, but *us*. Jesus speaks to us as he does to the Samaritan woman. Of course, we already know him, but perhaps we have not yet encountered him personally. We know who Jesus is, but perhaps we have not spoken with him, and we still have not recognized him as our Savior.

This season of Lent is a good occasion to draw near to him, to encounter him in prayer in a heart-to-heart dialogue, to speak with him, to listen to him. It is a good occasion to see his face in the face of a suffering brother or sister. In this way, we can renew in ourselves the grace of Baptism, and quench our thirst at the wellspring of the Word of God and of his Holy Spirit. And in this way, we can also discover the joy of becoming artisans of reconciliation and instruments of peace in daily life.

> May the Virgin Mary help us to draw constantly from grace, from the water that springs from the rock that is Christ the Savior, so that we may profess our faith with conviction and joyfully proclaim the wonders of the love of this merciful God, the source of all good.

Readings from the Fathers of the Church

Saint Ambrose,
Jesus is ready to give you to drink

For this reason the Lord says [to the Samaritan woman]: "If you knew the gift of God and who it is who says to you, 'Give me a drink,' you would have asked him, and he would have given you living water" (Jn 4:10). This is the water after which David's "soul has thirsted," the streams for which "the heart yearns" (cf. Ps 42:1–2), not being thirsty for the poison of serpents. Living water is spiritual grace, because it purifies the recesses of the mind and washes every sin from the soul and cleanses every error of hidden thoughts.

If you seek Jesus, abandon the "broken cisterns" (Jer 2:13). Christ is accustomed to sit not by the cisterns, but by the well. It was there that he was found by that Samaritan woman who believed, the one who wanted to draw water. Although you were supposed to go there in the morning, nevertheless even if you go later, even if you go at the sixth hour, you will be able to find Jesus there, weary from traveling (cf. Jn 4:6).

He has grown weary, but for you, because he has long been seeking you. It was your lack of faith, which lasted for so long, that wearied him. Nonetheless, he does not take offense: all that matters is that you come. He asks you for a drink, but he is ready to give you to drink. And he does not drink the water of a stream that flows away, but your salvation. He drinks your good dispositions, he drinks the cup, that is, the passion for the redemption of your faults, so that you, quenched with his sacred blood, may satisfy the thirst of this world.

The Road from Blindness to Light
Fourth Sunday of Lent

✝

John 9:1–41

35 When Jesus heard that they had thrown him out, he found him and said, "Do you believe in the Son of Man?" 36 He answered and said, "Who is he, sir, that I may believe in him?" 37 Jesus said to him, "You have seen him and the one speaking with you is he." 38 He said, "I do believe, Lord," and he worshiped him. 39 Then Jesus said, "I came into this world for judgment, so that those who do not see might see, and those who do see might become blind." 40 Some of the Pharisees who were with him heard this and said to him, "Surely we are not also blind, are we?" 41 Jesus said to them, "If you were blind, you would have no sin; but now you are saying, 'We see,' so your sin remains."

At the center of the Gospel this Fourth Sunday of Lent we find Jesus and a man blind from birth, who received sight after Christ healed him. The lengthy account opens with a blind man who begins to see, and it closes—and this is curious—with the alleged seers who remain blind in soul. The miracle is narrated by John in just two verses, because the

Evangelist does not want to draw attention to the miracle it-self, but rather to what follows, to the discussions it arouses, also to the gossip. So many times, a good work, a work of charity, arouses gossip and discussion, because there are some who do not want to see the truth. The Evangelist John wants to draw attention to something that also occurs in our own day when a good work is performed. The blind man who is healed is first interrogated by the astonished crowd—they saw the miracle and they interrogated him—then by the doctors of the law, who also interrogated his parents. In the end, the blind man who was healed attains to faith. And this is the greatest grace that Jesus grants him: not only to see, but also to know him, to see in him "the light of the world" (Jn 9:5).

While the blind man gradually draws near to the light, the doctors of the law on the contrary sink deeper and deeper into their inner blindness. Locked in their presumption, they believe that they already have the light; therefore, they do not open themselves to the truth of Jesus. They do everything to deny the evidence. They cast doubt on the identity of the man who was healed; they then deny God's action in the healing, taking as an excuse that God does not work on the Sabbath. They even doubt that the man was born blind. Their closure to the light becomes aggressive and leads to the expulsion from the temple of the man who was healed.

The blind man's journey on the contrary is a journey in stages that begins with the knowledge of Jesus' name. He does not know anything else about him; in fact, he says: "The man called Jesus made clay and anointed my eyes" (v. 11). Fol-lowing the pressing questions of the lawyers, he first considers him a prophet (v. 17) and then a man who is close to God (v. 31). Once he has been banished from the temple, expelled from society, Jesus finds him again and "opens his eyes" for the second time, by revealing his own identity to him: "I am the Messiah," he tells him. At this point the man who had been blind exclaims: "I do believe, Lord" (v. 38), and he prostrates himself before Jesus. This is a passage of the Gospel that makes evident the drama of the inner blindness of so many people, including our own, for sometimes we have moments of inner blindness.

Our lives are sometimes similar to that of the blind man who opened himself to the light, who opened himself to God, who opened himself to his grace. Sometimes unfortunately they are similar to those of the doctors of the law: from the height of our pride we judge others, and even the Lord! Today, we are invited to open ourselves to the light of Christ in order to bear fruit in our lives, to eliminate unchristian behaviors. We are all Christians, but we all—everyone—sometimes have unchristian behaviors, behaviors that are sins. We must repent of this, eliminate these behaviors in order to journey well along the way of holiness, which has its origin in Baptism. We too have been "enlightened" by Christ in Baptism, so that, as Saint Paul reminds us, we may act as "children of light" (Eph 5:8). The Sacrament of Baptism, in fact, requires the choice of living as children of the light and walking in the light.

If I were to ask you: "Do you believe that Jesus is the Son of God? Do you believe that he can change your heart? Do you believe that he can show reality as he sees it, not as we see it?

Do you believe that he is light, that he gives us the true light?" How would you answer?

Let us not forget this! I suggest that you read this passage from chapter 9 in the Gospel of Saint John several times. It will do you good, because you will thus see this road from blindness to light and the other evil road that leads to deeper blindness. Let us ask ourselves about the state of our own heart. Do I have an open heart or a closed heart? Is it opened or closed to God? Open or closed to my neighbor? We are always closed to some degree, which comes from original sin, from mistakes, from errors. We need not be afraid! Let us open ourselves to the light of the Lord; he awaits us always in order to enable us to see better, to give us more light, to forgive us.

Let us entrust this Lenten journey to the Virgin Mary, so that we too, like the blind man who was healed by the grace of Christ, may "come to the light," go forward toward the light and be reborn to new life.

Readings from the Fathers of the Church

Saint Augustine,
It is enough to recognize that one is blind

And Jesus said: Behold the day that distinguishes the light from the darkness. I have come into this world to make a judgment: "that those who do not see may see, and that those who see may become blind" (Jn 9:39). [. . .]

You have come so that they may see who do not see; this is right, because you are the light, because you are the day, because you free us from darkness; everyone accepts and understands this. But what is the meaning of that which follows: and that those who see may become blind? [. . .]

"Jesus said to them: 'If you were blind you would have no sin.'" [. . .] If you were blind, meaning if you realized that you are blind, if you admitted to being so, you would go to the doctor; if you were blind in this sense, you would have no sin, because I have come to take away sin; but since you say, "We see," your sin remains (Jn 9:40–41). Why? Because in deceiving yourselves that you see, you do not seek out the doctor and you remain in your blindness.

We Leave the Grave of Our Sins

Fifth Sunday of Lent

✝

John 11:1–45

39 Jesus said, "Take away the stone." Martha, the dead man's sister, said to him, "Lord, by now there will be a stench; he has been dead for four days." 40 Jesus said to her, "Did I not tell you that if you believe you will see the glory of God?"41 So they took away the stone. And Jesus raised his eyes and said, "Father, I thank you for hearing me. 42 I know that you always hear me; but because of the crowd here I have said this, that they may believe that you sent me." 43 And when he had said this, he cried out in a loud voice, "Lazarus, come out!" 44 The dead man came out, tied hand and foot with burial bands, and his face was wrapped in a cloth. So Jesus said to them, "Untie him and let him go."

The Gospel of this Fifth Sunday of Lent tells us of the resurrection of Lazarus. It is the culmination of the miraculous "signs" worked by Jesus: this act is too great, too clearly divine to be tolerated by the high priests, who, learning of the fact, decide to kill Jesus (cf. Jn 11:53).

Lazarus had already been dead four days before Jesus arrived; and what he said to the sisters Martha and Mary is engraved forever in the memory of the Christian community. Jesus speaks like this: "I am the resurrection and the life; he who believes in me, even if he dies, will live, and whoever lives and believes in me will never die" (vv. 25–26). With this word of the Lord we believe that the life of whoever believes in Jesus and follows his commandment will, after death, be transformed into new life, full and immortal. As Jesus is resurrected with his own body, though he does not return to an earthly life, so too will we be raised with our bodies, which will have been transfigured into glorified bodies. He expects us with the Father, and by the power of the Holy Spirit, who raised him, he will also raise those who are united to him.

Before the sealed tomb of his friend Lazarus, Jesus "cried with a loud voice: 'Lazarus, come out!' And the dead man came out, his hands and feet bound with bandages, and his face wrapped with a cloth" (cf. vv. 43–44). This cry is an imperative to all men, because we are all marked by death, all of us; it is the voice of the One who is master of life and wants that we all may "have it abundantly" (Jn 10:10). Christ is not resigned to the tombs that we have built for ourselves with our choice for evil and death, with our errors, with our sins. He is not resigned to this! He invites us, almost orders us, to come out of the tomb in which our sins have buried us. He calls us insistently to come out of the darkness of that prison in which we are enclosed, content with a false, selfish, and mediocre life. "Come out!" he says to us. "Come out!" It is an invitation to true freedom, to allow ourselves to be seized by these words of Jesus, who repeats them to each one of us today. It is an invitation to let ourselves be freed from the "bondages," from the bondages of pride. For pride makes of us slaves, slaves to ourselves, slaves to so many idols, so many things. Our resurrection begins here: when we decide to obey Jesus' command by coming out into the light, into life; when the mask falls from our face—we are frequently masked by sin, the mask must fall off!—and we find again the courage of our original face, created in the image and likeness of God.

Jesus' act of raising Lazarus shows the extent to which the power of God's grace can go and, thus, the extent of our conversion, our transformation. Listen carefully: there is no limit to divine mercy offered to everyone! There is no limit to divine mercy offered to everyone! Remember this sentence. And we can all say it together: "There is no limit to divine mercy, which is offered to all people!" Let us say it together: "There is no limit to divine mercy, which is offered to everyone!"

Let us remember that the Lord is always ready to remove the tombstone of our sins, which keeps us apart from him, the light of the living.

Readings from the Fathers of the Church

Saint Ambrose,
Jesus washes you with his tears

What we have read about Lazarus we should believe about every repentant sinner who, although he may give off an odor, nevertheless is cleansed by the ointment of a precious faith.

Faith, in fact, enjoys such favor that where the day before there was the stench of a corpse, the good scent now fills the whole house. [. . .]

Let us eat and let us celebrate, because this one "was dead, and has come back to life, he was lost, and has been found" (Lk 15:32). If some unbeliever should object: "Why does he eat with the sinners and the publicans?" (Mk 2:16) he will receive this answer: "They do not need a doctor who are sick, but they who are ill" (Mk 2:17). Then show the doctor your wound, so that you can be healed. Even if you do not show it, he knows about it, but for his part he is waiting to hear your voice. He erases your scars with his tears. [. . .]

May you deign, Lord Jesus, to come to this tomb of mine, to wash me with your tears, since in my parched eyes I do not have enough to be able to wash away my faults! If you weep for me, I shall be saved. If I am worthy of your tears, I shall remove the stench of all my sins. If I deserve to have you weep for me for a moment, you shall call me from the tomb of this body and say: "Come out," so that my thoughts may not remain in the restricted space of this body, but may go out to meet Christ and to live in the light, so that I may not think of the works of darkness, but of the works of light.

Who Am I
Before the Cross of Jesus?

Palm Sunday

+

Matthew 26:14–27:66

17 On the first day of the Feast of Unleavened Bread, the disciples approached Jesus and said, "Where do you want us to prepare for you to eat the Passover?" 18 He said, "Go into the city to a certain man and tell him, 'The teacher says, "My appointed time draws near; in your house I shall celebrate the Passover with my disciples."'" 19 The disciples then did as Jesus had ordered, and prepared the Passover.

This week begins with the festive procession with olive branches, when everyone welcomes Jesus. It is joyful and sorrowful at the same time. We celebrate the Lord's entrance into Jerusalem to the cries of his disciples, who acclaim him as King. Yet we also solemnly proclaim the Gospel account of his Passion. In this poignant contrast, our hearts experience in some small measure what Jesus himself must have felt in his own heart that day, as he rejoiced with his friends and wept over Jerusalem.

And these days will go on in the mystery of Jesus' death and Resurrection. So, as we joyfully acclaim our King, let us also think of the sufferings that he will have to endure in this week.

Jesus had clearly said this to his disciples: "If someone wants to come after me, he must deny himself, take up his cross and follow me" (Mt 16:24). He never promised honors and achievements. He had always warned his friends that this was to be his path, and that the final victory would be achieved through the Passion and the Cross. All this holds true for us too. Let us ask for the grace to follow Jesus faithfully, not in words but in deeds. Let us also ask for the patience to carry our own cross, not to refuse it or set it aside, but rather, in looking to him, to take it up and to carry it daily.

It will do us good to ask some questions: Who am I? Who am I, before my Lord? Who am I, before Jesus, who enters Jerusalem amid the enthusiasm of the crowd? Am I ready to express my joy, to praise him? Or do I stand back? Who am I, before the suffering Jesus?

We have just heard many, many names. The group of leaders, some priests, the Pharisees, the teachers of the law, who had decided to kill Jesus. They were waiting for the chance to arrest him. Am I like one of them?

We have also heard another name: Judas. Thirty pieces of silver. Am I like Judas? We have heard other names too: the disciples, who understand nothing, who fell asleep while the Lord was suffering. Has my life fallen asleep? Or am I like the disciples, who did not realize what it was to betray Jesus? Or like that other disciple, who wanted to settle everything with a sword? Am I like them? Am I like Judas, who feigns love and then kisses the Master in order to hand him over, to betray him? Am I a traitor? Am I like those people in power who hastily summon a tribunal and seek false witnesses: Am I like them? And when I do these things, if I do them, do I think that in this way I am saving the people?

Am I like Pilate? When I see that the situation is difficult, do I wash my hands and dodge my responsibility, allowing people to be condemned—or condemning them myself?

Am I like that crowd, which was not sure whether they were at a religious meeting, a trial, or a circus, and then chose Barabbas? For them it was all the same: it was more entertaining to humiliate Jesus.

Am I like the soldiers who strike the Lord, spit on him, insult him, who find entertainment in humiliating him?

Am I like the Cyrenian, who was returning from work, weary, yet was good enough to help the Lord carry his Cross?

Am I like those who walked by the Cross and mocked Jesus: "He was so courageous! Let him come down from the Cross and then we will believe in him!" Mocking Jesus . . .

Am I like those fearless women, and like the Mother of Jesus, who were there, and who suffered in silence?

Am I like Joseph, the hidden disciple, who lovingly carries the body of Jesus to give it burial?

Am I like the two Marys, who remained at the tomb, weeping and praying?

Am I like those leaders who went the next day to Pilate and said, "Look, this man said that he was going to rise again. We cannot let another fraud take place!" and who block life, who block the tomb, in order to maintain doctrine, lest life come forth?

Where is my heart? Which of these persons am I like?

May this question remain with us throughout this entire week.

Readings from the Fathers of the Church

Saint Caesarius of Arles,
Let us take up the cross, but follow him!

It seems hard, dearest brothers, and at first sight burdensome that the Lord has commanded in the Gospel: "If anyone wants to come after me, let him deny himself" (Mt 16:24). But it is not so hard, because he who gives this command also gives us the support needed to accomplish what he commands. [. . .]

Therefore, our Lord and Savior did not only say, "Let him deny himself," but added, "Take up his cross and follow me." What does it mean, "Let him take up his cross"? "Let him endure all that which is troublesome: thus will he follow me. When he begins to follow me in behaviors and in my precepts, there will be many who contradict him, hinder him; not only will they laugh at him, but they will even persecute him." I am not speaking only of the pagans, who are outside the Church, but also of those who seem to be inside the Church physically only, but are outside it on account of their evil deeds. They carry the name of Christian only, while they do nothing but persecute the good Christians. Such persons are in the members of the Church like the bad humors in the body. If, therefore, you desire to follow Christ, do not hesitate to carry his cross; bear with the wicked and do not let yourself be intimidated. [. . .]

Let us love the world: but let him come first who made the world. The world is beautiful, but more beautiful is he who created the world. The world is attractive, but even more beguiling is he who created the world.

A Love Without Measure
Holy Thursday

✝

John 15:1–15

9 "As the Father loves me, so I also love you. Remain in my love. 10 If you keep my commandments, you will remain in my love, just as I have kept my Father's commandments and remain in his love. 11 I have told you this so that my joy may be in you and your joy may be complete."

In the Gospel of Holy Thursday, Jesus speaks of the Father as a farmer who takes care of the branches in order to bring more fruit (cf. Jn 15:2). The secret of this caring is the profound union with Jesus: "I am the vine, you are the branches. Whoever remains in me, and I in him, will bear much fruit, because without me you can do nothing" (v. 5).

The fruits of this profound union with Christ are wonderful: our whole person is transformed by the grace of the Spirit: soul, understanding, will, affections, and even body, because we are united body and soul. We receive a new way of being; the life of Christ becomes our own: we are able to think like him, to act like him, to see the world and the things in it with the eyes of Jesus. And so, we are able to love our brothers and sisters, beginning with the poorest and those who suffer the most, as he did, and love them with his heart, and so bear fruits of goodness, of charity, and of peace in the world.

And the invitation to this union of us with Jesus comes from another even deeper union between Jesus and the Father: "As the Father loved me, I also loved you. Remain in my love" (v. 9). The word of Jesus is very strong, because he asks us to remain in the love that is between him and the Father. And that's because in life there may also be other loves. The world too proposes other loves to us: love of money, love of vanity, love of showing off; love of pride; love of power, and of doing many unjust things in order to have even more power. However, such cases are other loves; they are not of Jesus and are not of the Father. Christ asks us to abide in his love, which is the Father's love.

Indeed, the love with which Jesus loves us is the same as that with which the Father loved him. It's the same. We are loved with this great love. It is a great gift of love! For this very reason, Jesus admonishes us: "Please, abide in my love because it is the love of the Father. It is a great love." Recognizing the likely objection: "But, Lord, how can we abide in your love?" the Lord himself offers a concrete response: "If you keep my commandments, you will abide in my love, just as I have kept my Father's commandments and abide in his love."

This is the measure of love in which we must remain: observing the commandments that Jesus gives us, we will remain in the love of Jesus, which is love of the Father, without measure. Jesus teaches us the path of love: an open heart, loving without measure, and letting go of other loves, such as half-loving. This is not loving. The measure of love is to love without measure. The invitation that today Jesus addresses us with is this: "Obey the love of the Father, without other loves; obey this gift." But why does the Lord tell us these things? Yet once again, the answer is found in today's Gospel: "I have told you this so that my joy may be in you and your joy may be complete" (v. 11). Jesus invites us to love without measure, to obey the love of the Father, because he knows that only in this love is there the gift of joy, of great joy. This joy is a gift from the Lord. It fills us from within. It is as an anointing of the Spirit.

> **Let's ask ourselves: What gives me joy? Where do I instead delude myself to get joy? When am I able to love without limit? And when am I afraid to love like this?**

Readings from the Fathers of the Church

Saint Ignatius of Antioch,
From the love between Christ and the Father to our charity

I will not command you as if I were somebody. Although I am fettered in his name, I have not yet reached perfection in Jesus Christ. Only now am I beginning to learn, and I speak to you as to my fellow pupils. I need from you the anointing of faith, exhortation, patience, and magnanimity. But since charity does not allow me to remain silent with you, I want to urge you to communicate in harmony with the mind of God. And Jesus Christ, our indispensable life, is the thought of the Father, just as the bishops, put in place even to the ends of the earth, are in the thought of Jesus Christ.

It is fitting to proceed in agreement with the mind of the bishop, whereby in your unity and concordant love you may sing to Jesus Christ. And let each of you become part of one choir, so that in the harmony of your accord and taking in unity the tone from God, you may sing with one voice through Jesus Christ to the Father, so that he may hear you and acknowledge you, through good works, that you are the members of Jesus Christ. It is necessary for you to find yourselves in inseparable unity in order to be always partakers with God.

If in a short time I have had such familiarity with your bishop, which is not human but spiritual, all the more do I deem you blessed in being united with him as the Church is with Jesus Christ and Jesus Christ with the Father, so that all things may be harmonious in unity. Let no one deceive himself: he who is not near the altar is deprived of the bread of God. If the prayer of one or two has so much power, how much more does that of the bishop and of the whole Church! He who does not participate in the assembly is proud and has been judged. It is written: "God resists the proud." Let us take care not to oppose the bishop, in order that we may be subject to God.

I Will Not Leave You Orphaned; I Give You a Mother

Good Friday

✝

John 18:1–19:42

25 Standing by the cross of Jesus were his mother and his mother's sister, Mary the wife of Clopas, and Mary of Magdala. 26 When Jesus saw his mother and the disciple there whom he loved, he said to his mother, "Woman, behold, your son." 27 Then he said to the disciple, "Behold, your mother." And from that hour the disciple took her into his home.

This Good Friday Gospel is presented to us with Mary under the Cross. It's the second time that Mary is called "woman" by her Son. The first, in fact, was in Cana, when Jesus says to his Mother: "My hour has not come" (Jn 2:4). The second is this, under the Cross, when her Son gives her a child. Mary had authority in Cana, saying to the servants: "Whatever he tells you, do it" (Jn 2:5). But here it is Jesus who has authority: "Woman, behold your son." In that moment, Mary becomes a mother again. Her motherhood widens so broadly, it spreads to the whole Church and to all humanity. So much so that today we cannot think of Mary without thinking of her as Mother.

In this age, when there's a strong sense of being orphaned, this word has great importance. Jesus tells us: "I will not leave you orphaned; I give you a mother." This legacy is also our pride: we have a Mother, who is with us, who protects us, accompanies us, helps us, even in difficult times, in bad moments.

The tradition of the ancient Russian monks reminds us that in moments of spiritual turmoil, we can take refuge under the cloak of the Holy Mother of God. This advice is also found in the first antiphon Latin Mariana: *Sub tuum praesidium confugimus* ["Under thy protection we seek refuge"]. In this prayer, we find in the Mother the one who welcomes us and protects us, and takes care of us. But this motherhood of Mary goes further. It is contagious.

Through the ancient abbot Isaac, of the Monastery of Stella, we can understand that in addition to the "motherhood of Mary" there is also "a second motherhood," that of "our 'Holy Mother Church,' which engenders us in baptism, enables us to grow in her community," and has the very attitudes of motherhood: "meekness and goodness: Mother Mary and Mother Church know how to caress their children; they give tenderness."

Thinking of the Church without this motherhood is like thinking of a rigid organization, an organization without human warmth, orphaned. The Church, however, is mother and accepts us as a mother: Mother Mary, Mother Church.

That's not all. Isaac the Abbot adds yet another detail, which might "shock" us: even our soul is mother; there is even present within us a motherhood that is expressed in the attitudes of humility, acceptance, understanding, goodness, forgiveness, and tenderness.

And what does Mary teach us about this motherhood? This Gospel passage is more for contemplating than for mere reading: contemplate the Mother of Jesus, and with her contemplate the sign of contradiction of the Cross.

Jesus is the winner, yet is on the Cross. The Mother of God is aware of what he is experiencing, because he has lived all his life with a soul drawn out for him. We can imagine Mary following Jesus and he heard the comments that people said: "How great!"; "But this is not of God!"; "This is not a true believer!" Mary heard everything: all the words for and against Jesus. Yet, Mary has always been behind her Son—that's why we say she is the first disciple! At the Cross, Mary is standing, looking at her Son. And maybe she heard the comments: "Look, that is the mother of one of the three criminals." But she remained silent: she is the Mother, and her motherhood is in the fact that she did not deny the Son, but rather she showed her face for the Son. She showed up for him.

> What I am saying now are words to help contemplate this mystery in silence: in that moment, Mary gave birth to all of us, gave birth to the Church. With Mary, we too remain under the Cross in silence, to contemplate, to look. May it be the Holy Spirit who tells each of us what we need.

Readings from the Fathers of the Church

Isaac of Stella, The mothers of Christ:
Mary, the Church, the soul

There is in fact just one Christ, whole and sole, head and body. And this whole, which has one sole God in heaven and one sole mother on earth, is at the same time many children and one child. Just as in fact the head and the members are one sole child and many children, so too Mary and the Church are one mother and more than one mother, one virgin and more than one virgin. Both are mothers, both are virgins, both without lust conceived the same Spirit, both without sin gave offspring to God the Father. That, without any sin (cf. Heb 4:15), brought forth for the body the head; this, in the remission of all sins (cf. Acts 2:38), gave to the head a body. Both are mothers of Christ, but neither of the two without the other brings him forth whole and complete. For this reason, in the divinely inspired Scriptures that which is said in a universal sense about the virgin mother Church is correctly understood as valid in the singular sense for the virgin mother Mary, and that which applies in a special way to the virgin mother Mary applies in a general sense to the virgin mother Church. And when a text speaks of one or the other, what is affirmed applies equally and without distinction to the one and the other.

In the same way every faithful soul can be understood, in its own way, as bride of the Word of God, as mother and daughter and sister of Christ (cf. Mt 12:50), as both virginal and fruitful. Therefore, the Church in a universal sense, Mary in a special sense, and the faithful soul in a singular sense all participate in that which is said about the very Wisdom of God who is the Word of the Father. [. . .]

In the tabernacle of Mary's womb Christ dwelt for nine months; in the tabernacle of the Church's faith he dwells "until the end of the world" (Mt 28:20), in the conscience and in the love of the faithful soul he will dwell unto the ages of ages.

Stop, the Lord Is Risen!

Easter Sunday

✝

John 20:1–9

1 On the first day of the week, Mary of Magdala came to the tomb early in the morning, while it was still dark, and saw the stone removed from the tomb. 2 So she ran and went to Simon Peter and to the other disciple whom Jesus loved, and told them, "They have taken the Lord from the tomb, and we don't know where they put him." 3 So Peter and the other disciple went out and came to the tomb. 4 They both ran, but the other disciple ran faster than Peter and arrived at the tomb first; 5 he bent down and saw the burial cloths there, but did not go in. 6 When Simon Peter arrived after him, he went into the tomb and saw the burial cloths there, 7 and the cloth that had covered his head, not with the burial cloths but rolled up in a separate place.

Today the Church repeats, sings, shouts: "Jesus is Risen!" But why is this? Peter, John, the women went to the sepulchre and it was empty. He was not there. They went away with their hearts closed in sadness, the sadness of defeat: the Teacher, their Teacher, the One whom they loved so much had been put to death; he is dead. And there is no return from death. This is the defeat. This is the path of defeat, the path toward the sepulchre. But the angel says to them, "He is not here, he is Risen."

It is the first announcement: "He is Risen." And then the confusion, the closed hearts, the apparitions. But the disciples stayed locked in the Upper Room the entire day because they were afraid that what had happened to Jesus would happen to them. The Church does not cease to say before our losses, our closed and fearful hearts: "Stop, the Lord is Risen." But if the Lord is Risen, why is it that these things happen? Why is it that there is so much adversity: illness, human trafficking, human slavery, war, destruction, mutilation, vengeance, hatred? Where is the Lord then?

Yesterday, I phoned a young man with a grave illness, an educated young man, an engineer, and while talking to him, to give him a sign of faith, I said: "There are no explanations for what is happening to you. Look at Jesus on the Cross. God did this to his Son, and there is no other explanation." And he answered: "Yes, but he asked his Son and the Son said "yes." I was not asked if I wanted this."

This moves us. None of us is asked: "Are you happy with what is happening in the world? Are you willing to carry this cross further?" And the Cross goes forth and faith in Jesus comes down from it. Today, the Church continues to say: "Stop. Jesus is Risen." And this is not a fantasy. The Resurrection of Christ is not a celebration with many flowers. This is beautiful, but this is not it. It is something more. It is the mystery of the discarded stone which becomes the foundation of our existence. Christ is Risen. This is what it means.

In this throwaway culture where what is not needed is used and then disposed of, where what is not needed is thrown away, that stone—Jesus—the source of life, is discarded. And with faith in the Risen Christ, we too, pebbles on this earth of pain, tragedy, acquire meaning amid so many calamities. The sense to look beyond, the sense to say: "Look, there is no wall; there is a horizon, there is life, there is joy, there is the cross with this ambivalence. Look ahead, do not close within yourself. You pebble, acquire meaning in life because you are a pebble near that rock, that stone which the evil of sin discarded." What does the Church tell us today before so many tragedies? Simply this: the discarded stone is not really discarded. The pebbles which believe and stick to that stone are not discarded. They have meaning. It is with this sentiment that the Church repeats from the bottom of her heart: "Christ is Risen."

Let us think for a while, each of us, think about the daily problems, the illnesses we have been through or of one that a relative has; let us think about wars, human tragedies, and with simplicity, with a humble voice, without flowers, alone, before God, before us, let us say, "I do not know how this is, but I am certain that Christ is Risen and I have put a wager on it."

Brothers and sisters, this is what I wanted to say to you. Go home today repeating in your hearts: "Christ is Risen."

Readings from the Fathers of the Church

Saint Augustine,
The promise of eternal life

If we live, if we believe in him who is risen, he will give us things quite different from those who are loved here by them who do not love God, who, the less they love God, love all the more the things here below, and all the less the more they love him.

But let us see what he has promised us: not earthly and temporal riches, not honors and power of this world; as you see, all these things are granted also to the wicked, so that the good may not think them of great account.

Nor has he promised us the health of the body; not because he is not the one who grants it, but because, as you can see, he also grants it to the beasts.

Not a long life, as much as that can be called long which comes to an end. He has not promised to us believers, as if it were a great matter, longevity, extreme old age, which everyone desires before it comes but complains about when it is here.

Not the beauty of the body, which illnesses or the desired old age itself destroy. [. . .]

None of this is what has been promised to us by him who said: "Let him who believes in me come and drink; and from his breast shall flow fountains of living water" (Jn 7:37–38). He has promised us eternal life, where there is nothing we must fear, where we will be safe from all trouble, where we will not die, where there is no weeping over departures, where there is no waiting for arrivals.

The Sepulchre
Is Not the Last Word!

Easter Monday

✝

Matthew 28:8–15

8 Then they went away quickly from the tomb, fearful yet overjoyed, and ran to announce this to his disciples. 9 And behold, Jesus met them on their way and greeted them. They approached, embraced his feet, and did him homage. 10 Then Jesus said to them, "Do not be afraid. Go tell my brothers to go to Galilee, and there they will see me." 11 While they were going, some of the guard went into the city and told the chief priests all that had happened. 12 They assembled with the elders and took counsel; then they gave a large sum of money to the soldiers, 13 telling them, "You are to say, 'His disciples came by night and stole him while we were asleep.' 14 And if this gets to the ears of the governor, we will satisfy [him] and keep you out of trouble." 15 The soldiers took the money and did as they were instructed. And this story has circulated among the Jews to the present [day].

On this festive Monday known as "Monday of the Angel," the liturgy resounds the announcement of the Resurrection proclaimed yesterday: "Christ is Risen, Hallelujah!" In today's Gospel passage (Mt 28:8–15), we can hear the echo of the words the angel addressed to the women who had hastened to the sepulchre: *"Then go quickly and tell his disciples, 'He has been raised from the dead'"* (v. 28:7). We feel as if this invitation is also directed to us; to "hasten" and to "go" announce to the men and women of our times this message of joy and hope, of certain hope, because from the dawn of the third day, Jesus, who was crucified, is raised. Death no longer has the last word. Life does! This is our certainty. The sepulchre does not have the last word; it is not death, it is life! This is why we repeat "Christ is Risen" many times. Because in him, the sepulchre was overcome. Life was born.

In light of this event, which constitutes the true and real news of history and the cosmos, we are called to be new men and women in accordance with the Spirit, *confirming the value of life*. There is life! This is already the beginning of rebirth! We will be men and women of resurrection, men and women of life, if in the midst of the events that afflict the world—there are many of them today—in the midst of worldliness which distances us from God, we will know how to offer gestures of solidarity and gestures of welcome, strengthening the universal desire for peace and the hope for an environment free from degradation. These are common and human signs, which if supported and kept alive by faith in the Risen Lord, acquire a power that is well beyond our abilities. And this is so because Christ is alive and working in history through his Holy Spirit: he redeems our shortcomings and reaches each human heart and gives back hope to whoever is oppressed and suffering.

> **May the Virgin Mary, silent witness of the death and Resurrection of her Son Jesus, help us to be clear signs of the Risen Christ amid the affairs of the world, so that those who suffer tribulation and difficulties do not fall victim to pessimism, defeat, and resignation, but find in us many brothers and sisters who offer them support and solace. May our Mother help us to believe firmly in the Resurrection of Jesus: Jesus is Risen; he is alive here among us, and this is a worthy mystery of salvation with the ability to transform hearts and life. May she intercede especially for the persecuted and oppressed Christian communities which, in many parts of the world today, are called to a more difficult and courageous testimony.**

Readings from the Fathers of the Church

Melito of Sardis,
He is our resurrection

Now you lie dead;
he instead is risen from the dead
and has ascended to the heights of heaven.
The Lord, having clothed himself as man,
having suffered for him who was suffering
and having been bound for him who was fettered
and judged for him who was condemned

and buried for him who lay in the tomb,
rose from the dead and made his voice heard, crying:
"Who wants to stand in judgment against me?
Let him come forward (Is 50:8)!
It is I who have freed the condemned;
it is I who have brought life to the dead;
it is I who revive him who was buried.
Come now, then, come, all you of human lineage,
    immersed in sins. Receive the remission of sins. It is
    I, in fact, who am your remission, I am the Passover
    of salvation; I the Lamb immolated for you
    (Jn 1:29), I your ransom (Mt 20:28; Mk 10:45),
    I your life (Jn 11:25),
I your light (Jn 8:12),
I your salvation (Acts 4:12),
I your resurrection (Jn 11:25),
I your King" (Jn 18:37, 19:14; Mt 27:11). [. . .]

He is the Alpha and the Omega (Rev 1:8–21:6). He is
    the beginning and the end (Rev 21:6):
beginning unutterable and end incomprehensible.
    He is the Christ.
He is the King. He is Jesus:
the general,
the Lord,
he who is risen from the dead,
he who is seated at the right hand of the Father.
He bears the Father and is borne by the Father
    (Jn 10:30, 38): to Him be glory and power unto the
    ages. Amen.

Mercy Is a
True Form of Awareness

Second Sunday of Easter

✝

John 20:19–31

19 On the evening of that first day of the week, when the doors were locked, where the disciples were, for fear of the Jews, Jesus came and stood in their midst and said to them, "Peace be with you." 20 When he had said this, he showed them his hands and his side. The disciples rejoiced when they saw the Lord. 21 [Jesus] said to them again, "Peace be with you. As the Father has sent me, so I send you." 22 And when he had said this, he breathed on them and said to them, "Receive the holy Spirit. 23 Whose sins you forgive are forgiven them, and whose sins you retain are retained."

E ach Sunday we commemorate the Resurrection of the Lord Jesus, but in this period after Easter, Sunday takes on an even more illuminating significance. In the tradition of the Church, this Sunday, the first after Easter, was called [*Domenica*] *in albis*. What does this mean? The expression is meant to recall the rite performed by those who had received

Baptism at the Easter Vigil. Each of them would receive a white garment—*alba, bianca*—to indicate their new dignity as children of God. This is still done today: infants are offered a small symbolic garment, while adults wear a proper one, as we saw at the Easter Vigil. In the past, that white garment was worn for a week, until this Sunday, from which the name *in albis deponendis* is derived, which means the Sunday on which the white garment is removed. In this way, when the white garment was removed, the neophytes would begin their new life in Christ and in the Church.

In addition, in the Jubilee of the Year 2000, Saint John Paul II established that this Sunday be dedicated to Divine Mercy. Truly, it was a beautiful insight: it was the Holy Spirit who inspired him in this way. Just a few months ago we concluded the Extraordinary Jubilee of Mercy, and this Sunday we are invited to always hold firmly to the grace which comes from God's mercy.

Today's Gospel is the account of the Apparition of the Risen Christ to the disciples gathered in the Upper Room (Jn 20:19–31). Saint John writes that after greeting his disciples, Jesus says to them: "As the Father has sent me, so I send you" (v. 21). After saying this, he makes the gesture of breathing on them and adds: "Receive the Holy Spirit. Whose sins you forgive are forgiven them" (vv. 21–23). This is the meaning of the mercy that is presented on the very day of Jesus' Resurrection as the forgiveness of sins. The Risen Jesus passed on to his Church, as her first task, his own mission of bringing to all the concrete message of forgiveness. This is the first task: to announce forgiveness. This visible sign of his mercy brings with it peace of heart and joy of the renewed encounter with the Lord.

Mercy in the light of Easter enables us to perceive it as a *true form of awareness*. This is important: mercy is a true form of awareness. We know that it is experienced through many forms. It is experienced through the senses; it is experienced through intuition, through reason, and even other forms. It can also be experienced in mercy, because mercy opens the *door of the mind* in order to better understand the mystery of God and of our personal existence. Mercy enables us to understand that violence, rancor, vengefulness have no meaning, and the first victim is whoever feels these sentiments, because he deprives himself of his own dignity. Mercy also opens the *door of the heart* and allows one to express closeness, especially with those who are lonely and marginalized, because it makes them feel like brothers and sisters, and like children of one Father. It favors recognition of those who need consolation and helps one find the appropriate words, so as to give comfort.

Brothers and sisters, mercy warms the heart and makes it sensitive to the needs of brothers and sisters through sharing and participation. Thus, mercy requires everyone to be instruments of justice, reconciliation, and peace. Let us never forget that mercy is the keystone in the life of faith, and the concrete form by which we make Jesus' Resurrection visible.

May Mary, Mother of Mercy, help us to believe and joyfully experience all this.

Readings from the Fathers of the Church

Saint Ambrose,
The splendor of mercy

You have received white garments as a sign that you have taken off the wrapping of sins and have dressed yourself in the chaste garments of which the Prophet says: "Purify me with hyssop and I shall be clean; wash me and I shall be whiter than snow" (Ps 51:9). In fact, whoever is baptized appears purified. [. . .]

The Gospel itself says that when Christ was showing the glory of his Resurrection, his garments were white like snow. He whose sins are forgiven becomes whiter "than snow." As the Lord says through Isaiah: "Though your sins be as scarlet, they shall become white as snow" (Is 1:18).

The Church, with these garments that it has put on "through a washing of regeneration" (Ti 3:5), says in the words of the Canticle: "I am black, but beautiful, O daughters of Jerusalem" (cf. Song 1:5). Black on account of the frailty of the human condition, beautiful through grace. Black, because shaped by sinners, beautiful through the sacrament of faith. In catching sight of these garments, the daughters of Jerusalem would exclaim in amazement: "Who is this who comes forth all dressed in white? She was black, however has she suddenly become white?"

Christ, seeing his Church in white garments [. . .] or indeed seeing the soul clean and washed in the washing of regeneration, says: "How beautiful you are, my love, how beautiful you are! Your eyes are doves" (Song 4:1).

The Word of God, the Eucharist: They Fill Us with Joy

Third Sunday of Easter

+

Luke 24:13–35

30 And it happened that, while he was with them at table, he took bread, said the blessing, broke it, and gave it to them. 31 With that their eyes were opened and they recognized him, but he vanished from their sight. 32 Then they said to each other, "Were not our hearts burning [within us] while he spoke to us on the way and opened the scriptures to us?"

The Gospel from this Sunday, which is the Third Sunday of Easter, is that of the disciples of Emmaus (Lk 24:13–35). They were two of Jesus' disciples who, after his death and the Sabbath was past, leave Jerusalem and return, sad and dejected, to their village, which was named Emmaus. Along the way the Risen Jesus draws near to them, but they do not recognize him. Seeing them so sad, he first helps them to understand that the Passion and death of the Messiah were foreseen in the plan of God and announced in the Sacred Scriptures. And thus he rekindles a fire of hope in their hearts.

At that point, the two disciples experienced an extraordinary attraction to the mysterious man, and they invited him to stay with them that evening. Jesus accepted and went into the house with them. When, at table, he blessed the bread and broke it, they recognized him, but he vanished out of their sight, leaving them full of wonder. After being enlightened by the Word, they had recognized the Risen Jesus in the breaking of the bread, a new sign of his presence. And immediately they felt the need to go back to Jerusalem to tell the other disciples about their experience: that they had met the living Jesus and recognized him in the act of the breaking of the bread.

The road to Emmaus thus becomes a symbol of our journey of faith. The Scriptures and the Eucharist are the indispensable elements for encountering the Lord. We too often go to Sunday Mass with our worries, difficulties, and disappointments. [. . .] Life sometimes wounds us and we go away feeling sad, toward our "Emmaus," turning our backs on God's plan. We distance ourselves from God. But the liturgy of the Word welcomes us: Jesus explains the Scriptures to us and rekindles in our hearts the warmth of faith and hope, and in Communion he gives us strength. The Word of God, the Eucharist. Read a passage of the Gospel every day. Remember it well: read a passage from the Gospel every day, and on Sundays go to Communion, to receive Jesus. This is what happened to the disciples of Emmaus: they received the Word and they shared the breaking of bread. And from feeling sad and defeated they became joyful. Dear brothers and sisters, the Word of God and the Eucharist fill us with joy always. Remember it well! When you are sad, take up the Word of God. When you are down, take up the Word of God and go to Sunday Mass and receive Communion, to participate in the mystery of Jesus. The Word of God, the Eucharist: they fill us with joy.

Through the intercession of Most Holy Mary, let us pray that every Christian, in reliving the experience of the disciples of Emmaus, especially at Sunday Mass, may rediscover the grace of the transforming encounter with the Lord, with the Risen Lord, who is with us always. There is always a Word of God that gives us guidance after we slip; and through our weariness and disappointments, there is always a Bread that is broken that keeps us going on the journey.

Readings from the Fathers of the Church

Saint Justin, The Mass of the first Christians

We call this food "Eucharist," and no one else is allowed to participate in it except for him who believes as true the things we teach, and him who has bathed in the washing for the remission of sins and for regeneration, and who lives in the way that Christ taught. [. . .]

The apostles, in fact, in the memoirs that they left behind and that are called Gospels, hand down as they were commanded to do that Jesus, taking bread and giving thanks, said:

"Do this in memory of me, this is my body," and in the same way, taking the cup and giving thanks, said: "This is my blood" (cf. Mt 26:26–28), and had none but them take part. [. . .]

And on the day named after the sun, all of us gathering in one single place from the city and from the countryside make up one assembly where the memoirs of the apostles and the writings of the prophets are read as long as time permits; then, when the reader has finished, the presider admonishes and urges us to imitate these good things. Together we all stand and lift up prayers. As we have already said, after our prayer this bread, wine, and water are brought and he who presides, in the same way and as well as he is able, lifts up prayers and thanksgivings, and the people acclaim this by pronouncing the amen. The food over which the blessing has been said is then divided and distributed to each by the deacons, and is taken to those who are not present.

The Road from Blindness to Light

Fourth Sunday of Easter

✝

John 10:1–11

10 "A thief comes only to steal and slaughter and destroy; I came so that they might have life and have it more abundantly. 11 I am the good shepherd. A good shepherd lays down his life for the sheep."

The Evangelist John presents us, on this Fourth Sunday of the Easter Season, with the image of Jesus the Good Shepherd (Jn 10:1–11). In contemplating this page of the Gospel, we can understand the kind of relationship that Jesus had with his disciples: a relationship based on tenderness, love, mutual knowledge, and the promise of an immeasurable gift: "I came," Jesus said, "that they might have life and have it more abundantly" (v. 10). This relationship is the model for relations between Christians and for human relationships.

Today too, as in the time of Jesus, many put themselves forward as "shepherds" of our lives; but only the Risen One is the true Shepherd, who gives us life in abundance. I invite everyone to place their trust in the Lord, who guides us. But he not only guides us: he accompanies us, he walks with us. Let us listen to his Word with minds and hearts opened, to nourish our faith, enlighten our conscience, and follow the teaching of the Gospel.

On this Sunday let us pray for the shepherds of the Church, for all bishops, including the Bishop of Rome, for all priests, for everyone! We pray especially for the new priests of the Diocese of Rome, whom I ordained a short while ago in Saint Peter's Basilica. A greeting to these thirteen priests! May the Lord help us pastors always to be faithful to the Master, and wise and enlightened guides of the People of God, entrusted to us. I also ask you to please help us: help us to be good shepherds.

Once I read something very beautiful on how the People of God help bishops and priests to be good shepherds. It is a writing from Saint Caesarius of Arles, a father of the first centuries of the Church. He explained how the People of God must help the pastor, and he gave this example: when a calf is hungry it goes to the cow, its mother, to get milk. The cow, however, does not give it right away: it seems that she withholds it. And what does the calf do? It knocks with its nose at the cow's udder, so that the milk will come. It is a beautiful image! "So also you must be with your pastors," this saint said. "Always knock at their door, at their hearts, that they may give you the milk of doctrine, the milk of grace, and the milk of guidance."

And I ask you, please, bother the pastors, disturb the pastors, all of us pastors, so that we might give you the milk of grace, doctrine, and guidance. Bother them! Think of that beautiful image of the little calf, how it bothers its mother so that she might give it something to eat.

In imitation of Jesus, every pastor "will sometimes go before his people, pointing the way and keeping their hope vibrant. At other times, he will simply be in their midst with his unassuming and merciful presence. At yet other times, he will have to walk after them, helping those who lag behind" (*Evangelii Gaudium,* n. 31). May all pastors be so! But you must bother your pastors so that they may provide the guidance of doctrine and grace.

This Sunday is the World Day of Prayer for Vocations. In a previous message, I recalled that "every vocation, even within the variety of paths, always requires an exodus from oneself in order to center one's life on Christ and on his Gospel" (n. 2). Therefore, the call to follow Jesus is both exciting and challenging. In order that it may be realized, it is always necessary to enter into deep friendship with the Lord in order to live from him and for him.

Let us pray that also, in these times, many young people may hear the voice of the Lord, which is always in danger of being suffocated by the clamor of other voices. Let us pray for young people. Perhaps there is someone here in the square who hears the voice of the Lord calling him to the priesthood; let us pray for him, if he is here, and for all young people who are being called.

Readings from the Fathers of the Church

Saint Caesarius of Arles,
The faithful should go ahead and bother the priests

We can compare the priests in the Church to cows, while the symbol for the Christian people is calves. In fact, just as cows graze in fields and meadows, making the rounds of vineyards and olive groves and eating grass and leaves to prepare the milk with which they will feed their little calves, so also the priests, in reading the Word of God from the two mountains of the Sacred Scriptures, pick those "flowers" that are capable of offering spiritual milk to their children, joining the apostle Paul, who said "I gave you milk to drink, not solid food" (1 Cor 3:2). [. . .]

Yet consider, brothers, and observe that not only do the cows make their way toward their little calves, but the calves themselves come running to meet them and often push their faces against their mothers' udders so hard that at times, if the calves are big enough, it seems that they lift the bodies of their own mothers off the ground. But the cows willingly accept this annoyance to the extent to which they want to see their little calves grow up.

Good priests should also diligently desire and long for their children to bother them with continual requests for the salvation of their souls. In this way, while the children who knock at the door are lavished with divine grace, the reward of eternal life is prepared for the priests who open up the mysteries of the Holy Scriptures to them.

The Journey of Hope

Fifth Sunday of Easter

✝

John 14:2–6

2 "In my Father's house there are many dwelling places. If there were not, would I have told you that I am going to prepare a place for you? 3 And if I go and prepare a place for you, I will come back again and take you to myself, so that where I am you also may be. 4 Where [I] am going you know the way." 5 Thomas said to him, "Master, we do not know where you are going; how can we know the way?" 6 Jesus said to him, "I am the way and the truth and the life. No one comes to the Father except through me."

The Gospel passage for this Sunday is part of the speech Jesus gives after washing his disciples' feet (cf. Jn 13:31–17:26). Before the Passion, Jesus says to the apostles: "I will not leave you orphans" (Jn 14:18), I will not leave you alone, "I am going to prepare a place for you" (Jn 14:2). And he adds, "And if I go and prepare a place for you, I will come back again and take you to myself, so that where I am you also may be" (v. 3).

Jesus says: "I will come." This is the Christian's hope. The

Christian is a person of hope, who hopes the Lord will come back. But this is not just one personal hope, meant to be lived alone. The entire Church is waiting for the coming of Jesus. Jesus will return. We can then ask ourselves: How is my hope? Do I really think that the Lord will come again? Am I a person of hope?

Then Jesus goes on to say: "Where [I] am going you know the way" (v. 4). But Thomas replies: "Master, we do not know where you are going; how can we know the way?" To which Jesus says, "I am the way" (vv. 5-6).

This makes us think of the Christian life, which is a journey. But there are many ways to journey. First of all, there is that of not walking. A Christian who doesn't walk, who doesn't make his way, is an "unchristian" Christian, so to speak: he is a somewhat pagan Christian, standing there, standing still, immobile—he does not go forward in Christian life. He does not bring the Beatitudes to fruition in his life. He does not do works of mercy. He stands still. Pardon the word, but it is as if he were a "mummy," there, a "spiritual mummy." There are Christians who are "spiritual mummies" who don't do anything bad, but they don't do anything good. This way does not bear fruit; they are not fruitful Christians because they do not walk.

Then, there are some who walk and go astray, as we too often go astray. It is not a tragedy to go astray, for the Lord himself comes and helps us. In fact, the tragedy is in being stubborn and saying: "This is the way," and not letting the Lord's voice tell us: "This is not the way; turn around and go the right way." It is important to go back to the right path when we realize our errors, the mistakes we make, and not to be stubborn and always go astray, because this distances us from Jesus, because he is the way, but not the path astray.

Yet still, there are others who walk but don't know where they are going: they are misguided in Christian life, wanderers. They roam here and there, thus losing the beauty of drawing near to Jesus in life. In short, they lose their way because they roam. And so often this roaming, this misguided wandering, leads them to a life with no way out: too much wandering transforms life into a maze, and then they don't know how to get out. Thus, in the end, they have missed Jesus' call. They have no compass to find the way out and they wander, they roam, they search.

Then, there are others on the journey who are seduced by beauty, by something, and they stop midway, mesmerized by what they see, by that idea, by that proposal, by that landscape, and they stop. But Christian life is not charm, it is truth. It is Jesus Christ. As Saint Teresa of Avila said, speaking about this journey: "We are walking in order to arrive at the encounter with Jesus." In other words, just as a person walking to get somewhere doesn't stop because he likes a hotel, because he likes the landscape, but he goes onward, onward, onward. However, in this Christian life it is okay to pause, to look at the things I like, things of beauty—there are beautiful things and we must look at them, because God made them—but without stopping. Indeed, Christian life must continue. It is important to ensure that something beautiful, something peaceful, a peaceful life does not mesmerize me so as to stop me. Thus, there are many ways not to take the right path, because the righteous journey, the right way is Jesus.

Five minutes are enough to ask ourselves today, each one of us: How is my Christian journey, which I began in Baptism? Am I standing still? Have I gone astray? Am I constantly wandering, not knowing where to go spiritually? Do I stop at things I like: worldliness, vanity—so many things, no?—or do I always go forward, making the Beatitudes and the works of mercy tangible? It is good to ask ourselves this: it is a true examination of conscience! Essentially, we need to ask, How am I walking? Am I following Jesus? How am I doing on this Christian journey? Do I stop, do I do wrong, do I wander, do I stop in front of the things I like? Or do I follow Jesus?

Let us ask the Holy Spirit to teach us to walk correctly, always! And when we get tired, let us take a short rest and go on. Let us ask the Lord for this grace.

Readings from the Fathers of the Church

Epistle to Diognetus, Christians are like pilgrims

Christians live in Greek and barbarian cities, however it works out for each one. And in adapting to local customs in dress, food, and the rest, they bear witness to a method of social life that is wonderful and undoubtedly paradoxical. They live in their country, but as outsiders; they participate in everything as citizens and are detached from everything like foreigners.

Every foreign country is their country, and every country is foreign. They marry like everyone else and have children, but do not discard their newborns. They share a table together but not a bed. They are in the flesh but do not live according to the flesh (cf. 2 Cor 10:3). They dwell on earth but have their citizenship in heaven (cf. Phil 3:20). They obey the established laws, and in their lives they go beyond the laws. They love everyone, and by everyone they are persecuted. They are not known, and they are condemned. They are killed, and resume living. They are poor, and enrich many; they lack everything, and in everything abound! (cf. 2 Cor 6:9–10) [. . .]

To put it briefly, as the soul is in the body, so Christians are in the world. [. . .] The immortal soul inhabits a mortal dwelling. Christians also live as foreigners among the things that fall to corruption, awaiting incorruptibility in heaven.

Learn the Art of Loving

Sixth Sunday of Easter

+

John 14:15–26

23 Jesus answered and said to him, "Whoever loves me will keep my word, and my Father will love him, and we will come to him and make our dwelling with him. 24 Whoever does not love me does not keep my words; yet the word you hear is not mine but that of the Father who sent me. 25 I have told you this while I am with you. 26 The Advocate, the holy Spirit that the Father will send in my name—he will teach you everything and remind you of all that [I] told you."

Today's Gospel (Jn 14:15–26), the continuation of that of last Sunday, takes us back to the moving and dramatic moment of Jesus' Last Supper with his disciples. John the Evangelist gathers from the lips and heart of the Lord his last teachings, before his Passion and death. Jesus promises his friends, at that sad, dark moment, that after him, they will receive "another Paraclete" (v. 16). This word means another "Advocate," another Defender, another Counselor: "the Spirit of Truth" (v. 17); and he adds, "I will not leave you orphans; I will come to you" (v. 18). These words convey the joy of a new coming of Christ. He, Risen and glorified, dwells in the Father and at the same time comes to us in the Holy Spirit. And in his new coming, he reveals our union with him and with the Father: "You will realize that I am in my Father, and you are in me, and I in you" (v. 20).

Today, by meditating on these words of Jesus, we perceive with the sense of faith that we are the People of God in communion with the Father and with Jesus through the Holy Spirit. The Church finds the inexhaustible source of her very mission, which is achieved through love, in this mystery of communion. Jesus says in today's Gospel: "He who has my commandments and keeps them, he it is who loves me; and he who loves me will be loved by my Father, and I will love him and manifest myself to him" (v. 21). So, love introduces us to the knowledge of Jesus, thanks to the action of this "Advocate" which Jesus sent, that is, the Holy Spirit. Love for God and neighbor is the greatest commandment of the Gospel. The Lord today calls us to respond generously to the Gospel's call to love, placing God at the center of our lives and dedicating ourselves to the service of our brothers and sisters, especially those most in need of support and consolation.

If ever there is an attitude that is never easy, even for a Christian community, it is precisely how to love oneself, to love after the Lord's example and with his grace. Sometimes disagreements, pride, envy, divisions, all leave their mark even on the beautiful face of the Church. A community of Christians should live in the charity of Christ. Instead, it is precisely there that the evil one "sets his foot in." And sometimes we allow ourselves to be deceived. And those who pay the price are those who are spiritually weaker. How many of them—and you know some of them—how many of them have distanced themselves because they did not feel welcomed, did not feel understood, did not feel loved? How many people have distanced themselves, for example, from some parish or community because of the environment of gossip, jealousy, and envy they found there? Even for a Christian, knowing how to love is never a thing acquired once and for all. We must begin anew every day. We must practice it so that our love for the brothers and sisters we encounter may become mature and purified from those limitations or sins that render it incomplete, egotistical, sterile, and unfaithful. We have to learn the art of loving every day. Listen to this: Every day we must learn the art of loving; every day we must patiently follow the school of Christ. Every day we must forgive and look to Jesus, and do this with the help of this "Advocate," of this Counselor whom Jesus has sent to us—that is the Holy Spirit.

> May the Virgin Mary, the perfect disciple of her Son and Lord, help us to be more and more docile to the Paraclete, the Spirit of Truth, to learn every day how to love each other as Jesus loved us.

Readings from the Fathers of the Church

Saint Irenaeus of Lyon,
The Spirit, gift of the charity of Jesus

The Lord, after receiving the gift of eternal life from the Father himself, has given it in turn to those who take part in him, sending the Holy Spirit over all the earth. [. . .]

It is this same Spirit again whom he has given to the Church, sending from heaven the Paraclete over all the earth (cf. 1 Cor 12:4–7), there where the devil had been cast down like lightning, according to the word of the Lord (cf. Lk 10:18; Rev 12:9). Therefore, this dew from God is indispensable for us, so that we may not be burned up and so that where we have an accuser (cf. Rev 12:10) we may also have a defender. Because the Lord has entrusted to the Holy Spirit the man who belongs to him, the man who had fallen into the hands of the brigands; he had compassion on this man, he bandaged his wounds, giving two denarii (cf. Lk 10:30–35) so that, after receiving through the Spirit *the image and the inscription* (Mt 22:20; Mk 12:16; Lk 20:24) of the Father and the Son, we might fruitfully employ the denarius that has been entrusted to us, and give it back to the Lord multiplied (cf. Mt 25:14–30; Lk 19:12–27).

The Task of the Church

The Ascension of the Lord

+

Matthew 28:16–20

19 "Go, therefore, and make disciples of all nations, baptizing them in the name of the Father, and of the Son, and of the holy Spirit, 20 teaching them to observe all that I have commanded you. And behold, I am with you always, until the end of the age."

Today, we celebrate Jesus' Ascension into heaven, which took place forty days after Easter. The Gospel passage (Mt 28:16–20), which concludes the Gospel of Matthew, presents the moment of the Risen One's final farewell to his disciples. The scene is set in Galilee, the place where Jesus had called them to follow him and to form the first nucleus of his new community. Now those disciples have traversed the "fire" of the Passion and of the Resurrection; at the visit of the Risen Lord they prostrate themselves before him, although some remain doubtful. Jesus gives this frightened community the immense task of evangelizing the world; and he reinforces this responsibility with the command to teach and baptize in the name of the Father and of the Son and of the Holy Spirit (v. 19).

Jesus' Ascension into heaven thus constitutes the end of the mission that the Son received from the Father and the beginning of the continuation of this mission on the part of the Church. From this moment, from the moment of the Ascension, in fact, Christ's presence in the world is mediated by his disciples, by those who believe in him and proclaim him. This mission will last until the end of history, and every day will have the assistance of the Risen Lord, who assures: "I am with you always, until the end of the age" (v. 20).

His presence brings strength during persecution, comfort in tribulations, support in the difficult situations that the mission and the proclamation of the Gospel will encounter. The Ascension reminds us of Jesus' assistance and of his Spirit, which gives confidence, gives certainty to our Christian witness in the world. He reveals to us the reason for the Church's existence: the Church exists to proclaim the Gospel, *for this alone*! So too the joy of the Church is proclaiming the Gospel. The Church is all of us baptized people. Today we are called to better understand that God has given us the great dignity and responsibility of proclaiming him to the world, of making him accessible to all mankind. This is our dignity; this is the greatest honor of each one of us, of all the baptized!

On this Feast of the Ascension, as we turn our gaze toward heaven, where Christ has ascended and sits at the right hand of the Father, we strengthen our steps on earth so as to continue our journey—our mission of witnessing to and living the Gospel in every environment—with enthusiasm and courage. However, we are well aware that this does not depend first and foremost on our strengths, on our organizational abilities or human resources. Only with the light and strength of the Holy Spirit can we effectively fulfill our mission of leading others to know and increasingly experience Jesus' tenderness.

Let us ask the Virgin Mary to help us contemplate the heavenly benefits that the Lord promises us, and to become ever more credible witnesses to his Resurrection, to the true Life.

Readings from the Fathers of the Church

Saint Leo the Great,
Not only in the past, but in the present

Although it is proper of eternal life, not of this life, that God be all in all (cf. 1 Cor 15:28), nevertheless even now he dwells undivided within his temple, which is the Church (cf. Col 1:18), as he promised when he said: "Behold, I am with you all days, even until the end of the world" (Mt 28:20). [. . .]

All that the Son of God did and taught for the reconciliation of the world, we know not only in stories of past actions, but also by virtue of present works. The same one who was born from a virgin mother now makes the unsullied Church fruitful by the very work of the Spirit, producing by means of baptism a countless multitude of children of God. [. . .] Although he mainly says to blessed Peter: "Feed my sheep"

(Jn 21:17), it is still the same Lord who governs the care of all the shepherds: He nourishes those who come to the Rock with abundant and flowering pastures, so that many sheep, strengthened by the superabundant love of the Good Shepherd, who deigned to offer his life for his sheep (cf. Jn 10:15), in the same way as him may not be afraid to die for the name of their Shepherd.

With the Freedom of the Holy Spirit

Pentecost Sunday

✝

John 20:19–23

19 On the evening of that first day of the week, when the doors were locked, where the disciples were, for fear of the Jews, Jesus came and stood in their midst and said to them, "Peace be with you." 20 When he had said this, he showed them his hands and his side. The disciples rejoiced when they saw the Lord. 21 [Jesus] said to them again, "Peace be with you. As the Father has sent me, so I send you." 22 And when he had said this, he breathed on them and said to them, "Receive the holy Spirit."

The Feast of Pentecost commemorates the outpouring of the Holy Spirit on the apostles gathered in the Upper Room. Like Easter, this event took place on a preexisting Jewish feast and ended with a surprise. The Acts of the Apostles describes the signs and fruits of that extraordinary outpouring: the strong wind and tongues of fire; fear disappeared, leaving courage in its place; tongues melted and everyone understood the message. Wherever the Spirit of God reaches, everything is reborn and transfigured. Pentecost is the event that signals the birth of the Church and her public manifestation. Here, two features strike us: the Church *astounds* and *confuses*.

A fundamental element of Pentecost is *astonishment*. Our God is a God of *astonishment*, this we know. No one expected anything more from the disciples: after Jesus' death they were a small, insignificant group of defeated orphans of their Master. There occurred instead an unexpected event that astounded: the people were astonished because each of them heard the disciples speaking in their own tongues, telling of the great works of God (cf. Acts 2:6-11). The Church born at Pentecost is an astounding community because, with the force of her arrival from God, a new message is proclaimed—the Resurrection of Christ—with a new language: the universal one of love. A new proclamation: Christ lives, he is Risen; a new language: the language of love. The disciples are adorned with power from above and speak with courage—only minutes before they all were cowardly, but now they speak with courage and candor, with the freedom of the Holy Spirit.

Thus, the Church is called into being forever: capable of astounding while proclaiming to all that Jesus Christ has conquered death, that God's arms are always open, that his patience is always there awaiting us in order to heal us, to forgive us. The Risen Jesus bestowed his Spirit on the Church for this very mission.

Take note: if the Church is alive, she must always surprise.

It is incumbent upon the living Church to astound. A Church which is unable to astound is a Church that is weak, sick, dying, and that needs admission to the intensive care unit as soon as possible!

Some in Jerusalem would have liked for Jesus' disciples, frozen in fear, to remain locked inside so as not to create *confusion*. Even today, many would like this from the Christians. Instead, the Risen Lord pushes them into the world: "As the Father has sent me, so I send you" (Jn 20:21). The Church of the Pentecost is a Church that won't submit to being powerless, too "distilled." No, she doesn't submit to this! She doesn't want to be a decoration. She is a Church that doesn't hesitate to go out, meet the people, proclaim the message that's been entrusted to her, even if that message disturbs or unsettles the conscience, even if that message perhaps brings problems and sometimes leads to martyrdom. She is born one and universal, with a distinct identity, but open, a Church that embraces the world but doesn't seize it; she sets it free, but embraces it like the colonnade in this square: two arms that open to receive, but that don't close to detain. We Christians are free, and the Church wants us free!

We turn to the Virgin Mary, who on that Pentecost morning was in the Upper Room, the Mother with her children. In her, the force of the Holy Spirit truly accomplished "great things" (Lk 1:49). She herself said so. May she, the Mother of the Redeemer and Mother of the Church, obtain through her intercession a renewed outpouring of God's Spirit upon the Church and upon the world.

Readings from the Fathers of the Church

Tertullian,
The apostles and the power of the Holy Spirit

Having received the power of the Holy Spirit that had been promised for the working of miracles and for eloquence and after bearing witness in Judea to faith in Jesus Christ and establishing communities there, the apostles went out into the world and proclaimed to the nations the same doctrine and the same faith. And as they had done in Judea, they founded Churches in each city. From these all the other Churches afterward received the grafting of the faith and the seeds of doctrine, and they still receive them, in order to be Churches. [. . .] Unity is shown by the exchange of peace and by the title of "brother," and by particular signs of reciprocal hospitality. [. . .]

[The Lord] once said: "I have many things still to tell you, but you cannot yet bear them" (Jn 16:12); he nevertheless added: "When the Spirit of truth comes, he will lead you into all truth" (v. 13), showing thereby that nothing was unknown to those who had received all truth thanks to the Spirit of truth, according to his promise. And above all he kept his promise, since the Acts of the Apostles bears witness to the descent of the Holy Spirit (cf. Acts 2:1–4).

The Love That Is God
The Most Holy Trinity

+

John 3:16–18

16 For God so loved the world that he gave his only Son, so that everyone who believes in him might not perish but might have eternal life. 17 For God did not send his Son into the world to condemn the world, but that the world might be saved through him.

Today we celebrate the Solemnity of the Holy Trinity, which leads us to contemplate and worship the divine life of the Father, the Son, and the Holy Spirit, a life of communion and perfect love, origin and aim of all the universe and of every creature: God. We also recognize in the Trinity the model for the Church, in which we are called to love each other as Jesus loved us. And love is the concrete sign that demonstrates faith in God the Father, Son, and Holy Spirit. And love is the badge of the Christian, as Jesus told us: "This is how all will know that you are my disciples, if you have love for one another" (Jn 13:35). It's a contradiction to think of Christians who hate. It's a contradiction. And the devil always seeks this: to make us hate, because he's always a troublemaker; he doesn't know love. God is love!

We are all called to witness and proclaim the message that "God is love," that God isn't far and insensitive to our human affairs. He is close to us, always beside us, walking with us to share our joys and our sorrows, our hopes and our struggles. He loves us very much, and for that reason he became man. He came into the world not to condemn it, but so the world would be saved through Jesus (cf. Jn 3:16–17). And this is the love of God in Jesus, this love that is so difficult to understand but that we feel when we draw close to Jesus. He always forgives us, he always awaits us, he loves us so much. And we feel the love of Jesus and the love of God.

The Holy Spirit, gift of the Risen Jesus, conveys divine life to us and thus lets us enter into the dynamism of the Trinity, which is a dynamism of love, of communion, of mutual service, of sharing. A person who loves others for the very joy of love is a reflection of the Trinity. A family in which each person loves and helps one another is a reflection of the Trinity. A parish in which each person loves and shares spiritual and material effects is a reflection of the Trinity.

Today's Gospel (Jn 3:16–18) "sets the stage" for Nicodemus, who, while playing an important role in the religious and civil community of the time, has not ceased seeking God. He did not think, *I have arrived*; he did not cease seeking God; and now he has perceived the echo of his voice in Jesus. In the nighttime dialogue with the Nazarene, Nicodemus finally understood that he had *already* been sought and awaited by God, that he was personally loved by him. God always seeks

us first, awaits us first, loves us first. He is like the flower of
the almond tree; thus says the prophet: "It blooms first" (cf.
Jer 1:11–12). In fact, Jesus speaks to him in this way: "God so
loved the world that he gave his only Son, so that everyone
who believes in him might not perish but might have eternal
life" (Jn 3:16). What is this eternal life? It is the immeasurable
and freely given love of the Father, which Jesus gave on the
Cross, offering his life for our salvation. And this love with
the action of the Holy Spirit has shined a new light on the
earth and into every human heart that welcomes him, a light
that reveals the dark corners, the hardships that impede us
from bearing the good fruits of charity and of mercy.

> May the Virgin Mary, perfect creation of the Trinity, help us
> to make our whole lives, in small gestures and more impor-
> tant choices, an homage to God, who is Love.

Readings from the Fathers of the Church

Saint Augustine,
The shape of love

Love lies in this. Here is how the love of God has been made
manifest in us: that God sent his only begotten Son into this
world, so that we may live through him. In this is love, not in
the fact that we have loved, but in the fact that he himself has
loved us.

We were not the first to love him: in fact, he has loved us
for this, that we might love him. And God sent his Son as
propitiator of our sins: propitiator, sacrificer. He immolated

the victim for our sins. Where did he find the victim? Where did he find that pure victim which he wanted to offer? He did not find it, but offered himself. Dearly beloved, if God has so loved us, we should also love one another (cf. 1 Jn 4:9–11). "Peter," he said, "do you love me?" And he replied, "I love you."

"Feed my sheep" (Jn 21:15–17).

"No one has ever seen God" (1 Jn 4:12). God is invisible; he must not be sought with the eyes, but with the heart. [. . .] No one can get an idea of God by following the judgment of the eyes. He would get the idea of an immense form, or would extend into space an immeasurable size, like this light that strikes our eyes and that he spreads endlessly in all directions; or he would get an idea of God as an old man with a venerable appearance. You should not think this way. If you want to see God, you already have access to the right idea: God is love.

What face does love have? What shape, what size, what feet, what hands? No one can say. And yet it has feet, that lead to the Church; it has hands, that give to the poor; it has eyes, with which one comes to know the one who is in need; as the psalm says: "Blessed is he who considers the poor and the indigent" (Ps 41:2).

A Gift Without Measure

Eleventh Week of Ordinary Time

✝

John 6:51–58

51 "I am the living bread that came down from heaven; whoever eats this bread will live forever; and the bread that I will give is my flesh for the life of the world."

I n many countries we are celebrating the Solemnity of the Body and Blood of Christ—the Latin name is often used: *Corpus Domini* or *Corpus Christi*. Every Sunday the ecclesial community gathers around the Eucharist, the Sacrament instituted by Jesus at the Last Supper. Nevertheless, each year we joyfully celebrate the feast dedicated to this mystery, which is central to the faith, in order to fully express our adoration to Christ, who offers himself as the food and drink of salvation.

The Gospel of John presents the discourse on the "bread of life," held by Jesus in the Synagogue of Capernaum, in which he affirms, "I am the living bread that came down from heaven; whoever eats this bread will live forever; and the bread that I will give is my flesh for the life of the world" (Jn 6:51).

Jesus underlines that he has not come into this world to give something, but to give himself, his life, as nourishment for those who have faith in him. This, our communion with the Lord, obliges us, his disciples, to imitate him, making our existence, through our behavior, bread broken for others, as the Teacher has broken the bread that is truly his flesh. Indeed, this means for us generous conduct toward our neighbor, thereby demonstrating the attitude of giving life for others.

Every time we participate in Holy Mass and we are nourished by the Body of Christ, the presence of Jesus and of the Holy Spirit acts in us, shaping our hearts, communicating an interior disposition to us that translates into conduct according to the Gospel. Above all, docility to the Word of God, then fraternity among ourselves, the courage of Christian witness, creative charity, the capacity to give hope to the disheartened, to welcome the excluded. In this way the Eucharist fosters a mature Christian lifestyle. The charity of Christ, welcomed with an open heart, changes us, transforms us, renders us capable of loving not according to human measure, always limited, but according to the measure of God. And what is the measure of God? Without measure! The measure of God is without measure. Everything! Everything! Everything! It's impossible to measure the love of God: it is without measure!

And so, we become capable of loving even those who do not love us. And this is not easy. To love someone who doesn't love us . . . It's not easy! Because if we know that a person doesn't like us, then we also tend to bear ill will. But no! We must love even someone who doesn't love us! Opposing evil with good, with pardon, with sharing, with welcome. Thanks to Jesus and to his Spirit, even our life becomes "bread broken" for our brothers and sisters. In living like this, we discover true joy! The joy of making oneself a gift, of reciprocating the great gift that we have first received, without merit of our own. This is beautiful: our life is made a gift! This causes us to imitate Jesus. I wish to remind you of these two things. First: the measure of God's love is love without measure. Is this clear? And our life, with the love of Jesus, received in the Eucharist, is made a gift. As was the life of Jesus. Don't forget these two things: the measure of the love of God is love without measure. And following Jesus, we, with the Eucharist, make of our life a gift.

Jesus, Bread of eternal life, came down from heaven and was made flesh thanks to the faith of Mary Most Holy. After having borne him in herself with ineffable love, she followed him faithfully unto the Cross and to the Resurrection.

Let us ask Our Lady to help us rediscover the beauty of the Eucharist, to make it the center of our life, especially at Sunday Mass and in adoration.

Readings from the Fathers of the Church

Saint Cyprian, *The daily bread of life*

When we ask in our prayer "Give us our daily bread," [. . .] the bread of life is Christ, and this bread is not everyone's, but is ours. And just as we say "our Father," in that he is the father of Christians and believers, so likewise we say "our bread," because Christ is bread for us who unite ourselves with his body. We who are in Christ and receive his Eucharist every day as food for salvation, let us ask that this bread be given to us every day, so that we may not be separated from the body of Christ. [. . .] Therefore let us ask every day that we be given our bread, meaning Christ, so that by remaining in Christ and living in Him, we may not depart from his sanctification and from his body.

In reality, one can understand this in another way, which is that of asking for ourselves only the food and sustenance for each day. [. . .] God teaches that he is truly perfect who hides away for himself a treasure in heaven, after selling his possessions and distributing the proceeds to the poor. One can say that he truly follows and imitates the glory of the Passion who, free from every good and unencumbered, is not entangled in the snares of any inheritance, but loosed from all bonds and ready for service places himself, like the possessions he has already sold, at the feet of the Lord.

The Mission Is Not
Under the Banner of Tranquillity
Twelfth Sunday of Ordinary Time

✝

Matthew 10:26–33

26 "Therefore do not be afraid of them. Nothing is concealed that will not be revealed, nor secret that will not be known. 27 What I say to you in the darkness, speak in the light; what you hear whispered, proclaim on the housetops. 28 And do not be afraid of those who kill the body but cannot kill the soul; rather, be afraid of the one who can destroy both soul and body in Gehenna."

In today's Gospel (Mt 10:26–33) the Lord Jesus, after having called and sent the disciples on mission, teaches them and prepares them to face the trials and persecutions they will have to endure. Going on mission is not like tourism, and Jesus cautions them, "You will find persecutions." Then he exhorts them: "Do not be afraid of them. Nothing is concealed that will not be revealed. . . . What I say to you in the darkness, speak in the light. . . . And do not be afraid of those who kill the body but cannot kill the soul" (Mt 10:26–28).

They can only kill the body; they do not have the power to kill souls: do not fear this. Jesus' dispatch [of the disciples] on mission does not guarantee their success, just as it does not protect them from failure and suffering. They have to take into account both the possibility of rejection and that of persecution. This is somewhat frightening, but it is the truth.

The disciple is called to conform his life to Christ, who was persecuted by men, knew rejection, abandonment, and death on the Cross. There is no Christian mission marked by tranquillity! Difficulties and tribulations are part of the work of evangelization, and we are called to find in them the opportunity to test the authenticity of our faith and of our relationship with Jesus. We must consider these difficulties as the opportunity to be even more a missionary and to grow in that trust toward God, our Father, who does not abandon his children during the storm. Amid the difficulties of Christian witness in the world, we are not forgotten but always assisted by the attentive concern of the Father. For this reason, in today's Gospel, a good three times Jesus reassures the disciples, saying: "Do not fear!"

Even in our day, brothers and sisters, persecution against Christians is present. We pray for our brothers and sisters who are persecuted, and we praise God because, in spite of this, they continue to bear witness to their faith with courage and faithfulness. Their example helps us to not hesitate in taking the position in favor of Christ, bearing witness bravely in everyday situations, even in apparently peaceful contexts. In effect, a form of trial can also be the absence of hostility and tribulation. Besides [sending us out] as "sheep in the midst of wolves" (Mt 10:16), the Lord, even in our times, sends us out as sentinels in the midst of people who do not want to be woken from their worldly lethargy, which ignores the Gospel's words of truth, building for themselves their own ephemeral truths. And if we go to or live in these contexts, and we proclaim the words of the Gospel, this is bothersome, and they will look at us unkindly.

But in all this, the Lord continues to tell us, as he did the disciples of his time: "Do not fear!" Let us not forget these words: always, when we experience any tribulation, any persecution, anything that causes us to suffer, let us listen to the voice of Jesus in our hearts: "Do not fear! Do not fear! Go forth! I am with you!" Do not fear those who mock you and mistreat you and do not fear those who ignore you or respect you "to your face" but fight the Gospel "behind your back." There are so many who smile to our face then fight the Gospel behind our backs. We all know them. Jesus does not leave us alone, because we are precious to him. That is why he does not leave us alone. Each one of us is precious to Jesus, and he accompanies us.

May the Virgin Mary, example of humility and courageous adherence to the Word of God, help us to understand that success does not count in the witness of faith, but rather faithfulness—faithfulness to Christ—recognizing in any circumstance, even the most problematic, the inestimable gift of being his missionary disciples.

Readings from the Fathers of the Church

Tertullian,
Persecution sows conversion

But come now, good rulers, much more highly regarded by the people if you immolate Christians. Crucify us, torture us, condemn us, crush us: the proof of our innocence lies in your injustice! It is for this reason that God suffers that we should suffer these things. Because recently also in condemning us to prostitution rather than to the beasts, you have confessed that the loss of modesty is for us more atrocious than any condemnation and any kind of death.

And yet you achieve nothing with your most unjust cruelties: they are instead an attraction for our "sect." We become more numerous every time you mow us down. The blood of Christians is a seed of conversion. [. . .]

Who, in fact, at the sight of such stubbornness does not feel disturbed and does not seek what may be at the bottom of this mystery? Who, when he has discovered it, does not draw near, and when he has drawn near, does not desire to suffer, in order to gain the full grace of God, in order to obtain complete forgiveness in exchange for his own blood? Every fault, in fact, is remitted with that sacrifice. And this is why we thank you for your sentences. The difference between divine things and human is that, while we are condemned by you, we are acquitted by God.

A Transparent Heart
Thirteenth Sunday of Ordinary Time

✝

Matthew 10:37–42

37 "Whoever loves father or mother more than me is not worthy of me, and whoever loves son or daughter more than me is not worthy of me; 38 and whoever does not take up his cross and follow after me is not worthy of me. 39 Whoever finds his life will lose it, and whoever loses his life for my sake will find it. 40 Whoever receives you receives me, and whoever receives me receives the one who sent me."

Today's liturgy presents to us the last lines of the missionary discourse in chapter 10 of the Gospel of Matthew (vv. 37–42), by which Jesus instructs the twelve apostles at the moment in which, for the first time, he sends them on mission to the villages of Galilee and Judea. In this final part, Jesus underscores two essential aspects of the life of a missionary disciple: the first, that his *bond with Jesus is stronger* than any other bond; the second, that the *missionary brings not himself, but Jesus,* and through him the love of the heavenly Father. These two aspects are connected, because the more

Jesus is at the center of the heart and of the life of a disciple, the more this disciple is "transparent" to his presence. The two go hand in hand.

"Whoever loves father or mother more than me is not worthy of me" (v. 37), Jesus says. A father's affection, a mother's tenderness, the gentle friendship among brothers and sisters, all this, even while being very good and valid, cannot be placed before Christ. Not because he wants us to be heartless and ungrateful, but rather, on the contrary, because the condition of a disciple demands a priority relationship with the teacher. Any disciple, whether a layman or laywoman, a priest or a bishop, requires an all-absorbing relationship. Perhaps the first question that we must ask a Christian is: Do you meet with Jesus? Do you pray to Jesus?

Those who allow themselves to be drawn into this bond of love and of life with the Lord Jesus become his representatives, his "ambassadors," above all in the way of being, of living. To the point that Jesus himself, in sending his disciples on mission, says to them: "He who receives you receives me, and he who receives me receives him who sent me" (Mt 10:40). It is important that the people perceive that for that disciple Jesus is truly "the Lord"; he is truly the center of his or her life, the everything of life.

It does not matter then if, as for every human being, he or she has limitations and even makes mistakes—as long as he or she has the humility to recognize them; the important thing is that no one has a duplicitous heart, which is dangerous. I am a Christian; I am a disciple of Jesus; I am a priest; I am a bishop, but I have a duplicitous heart. No, this is not okay.

One must not have a duplicitous heart, but rather a simple, cohesive heart; [one must] not keep one foot in two shoes, but be honest with oneself and with others. Duplicity is not Christian. This is why Jesus prays to the Father so that the disciples may not fall prey to the worldly spirit. You are either with Jesus, with the spirit of Jesus, or you are with the spirit of the world.

Here, our experience as priests teaches us something very beautiful, something very important: it is precisely this welcoming of the holy, faithful People of God, it is precisely that "cup of cold water" (v. 42) that the Lord speaks of today in the Gospel, given with affectionate faith, which helps you to be a good priest! There is a reciprocity in mission too: if you leave everything for Jesus, the people recognize the Lord in you; at the same time, it helps you to convert each day to him, so as to renew and purify yourself from compromises and to overcome temptations. The closer a priest is to the People of God, the closer will he feel to Jesus, and the closer a priest is to Jesus, the closer will he feel to the People of God.

The Virgin Mary felt in the first person what it means to love Jesus by separating herself from him, giving new meaning to family ties, beginning with faith in him. With her maternal intercession, may she help us to be free and happy missionaries of the Gospel.

Readings from the Fathers of the Church

Saint Augustine,
Being little Christs

On how Christ is formed in the believer through the faith conceived in the inner man who, as a result, is called to the freedom of grace. It should be noted that this takes place in the one who is meek and humble of heart, who does not glory in his own merits, which do not exist, but in the grace in which all merit has its origin. Such a man is called the least of his own, meaning another of himself, by him who said: "Whenever you did this to one of the least of my [brothers], you did it to me" (Mt 25:40). Christ is in fact formed in the one who takes on conformity with Christ, and he takes on conformity with Christ who adheres to him with spiritual love. The imitation of Christ leads the Christian to become what Christ is, insofar as his condition allows. This is what John affirms: "He who says he dwells in Christ should behave as he behaved" (cf. 1 Jn 2:6). [. . .]

If therefore [Saint Paul] says: "I am in labor with you once again until Christ be formed in you" (cf. Gal 4:19), he does not say this in reference to the beginning of faith, when they were born in it, but in relation to how they are growing strong and becoming perfect. Paul describes this birth in another text, where he says: "My daily combat, my pressing concern for all the Churches. Who is weak, and I am not made weak? Who suffers scandal, and I am not inflamed?" (cf. 2 Cor 11:28–29).

Jesus Does Not Take Away
Our Cross, but Carries It with Us

Fourteenth Sunday of Ordinary Time

✝

Matthew 11:25–30

28 "Come to me, all you who labor and are burdened, and I
will give you rest. 29 Take my yoke upon you and learn
from me, for I am meek and humble of heart; and you will
find rest for yourselves. 30 For my yoke is easy, and my burden light."

In today's Gospel, Jesus says: "Come to me, all you who
labor and are burdened, and I will give you rest" (Mt 11:28).
The Lord does not reserve this invitation for certain friends
of his. No, he addresses it to "all" those who are weary and
overwhelmed by life. And who could feel excluded from this
invitation? The Lord knows how arduous life can be. He
knows that many things weary the heart: disappointments
and wounds of the past, burdens to carry and wrongs to bear
in the present, uncertainties and worries about the future.

In the face of all this, Jesus' first word is an invitation, a
call to move and respond: "Come." The mistake, when things

go wrong, is to stay where we are, lying there. It seems obvious, but how difficult it is to respond and open ourselves! It is not easy. In dark times it feels natural to keep to ourselves, to ruminate over how unfair life is, over how ungrateful others are, how mean the world is, and so on. We all know it. We have had this awful experience a few times. But in this way, locked up inside ourselves, we see everything as grim. Then we even grow accustomed to sadness, which becomes like our home. That sadness overcomes us. It is a terrible thing. Jesus, however, wants to pull us out of this "quicksand," and thus says to each one: "Come!—Who?—You, you, you." The way out is in connecting, in extending a hand and lifting our gaze to those who truly love us.

In fact, it is not enough to come out of ourselves; it is important to know where to go. Because many aims are illusory: they promise comfort and distract just a little; they guarantee peace and offer amusement, then leave us with the loneliness there was before. They are "fireworks." Therefore, Jesus indicates where to go: "Come *to me*." And many times, in the face of a burden of life or a situation that saddens us, we try to talk about it with someone who listens to us, with a friend, with an expert. . . . This is a great thing to do. But let us not forget Jesus. Let us not forget to open ourselves to him and to recount our life to him, to entrust people and situations to him. Perhaps there are "areas" of our life which we have never opened up to him and which have remained dark, because they have never seen the Lord's light. Each of us has our own story. And if someone has this dark area, seek out Jesus; go to a missionary of mercy; go to a priest; go. . . . But go to Jesus, and tell Jesus about this. Today he says to each one: "Take courage; do not give in to life's burdens; do not close yourself off in the face of fears and sins. Come to me!"

He awaits us; he always awaits us. Not to magically resolve problems, but to strengthen us amid our problems. Jesus does not lift the burdens from our life, but the anguish from our heart; he does not take away our cross, but carries it with us. And with him every burden becomes light (cf. v. 30), because he is the comfort we seek.

When Jesus enters life, peace arrives, the kind that remains even in trials, in suffering. Let us go to Jesus; let us give him our time; let us encounter him each day in prayer, in a trusting and personal dialogue; let us become familiar with his Word; let us fearlessly rediscover his forgiveness; let us eat of his Bread of Life. We will feel loved; we will feel comforted by him.

It is he himself who asks it of us. He almost insists on it. He repeats it again at the end of today's Gospel: "Learn from me, and you will find rest for yourselves" (cf. v. 29). And thus, let us learn to go to Jesus and, in the summer months, as we seek a little rest from what wearies the body, let us not forget to find true comfort in the Lord. May the Virgin Mary our Mother, who always takes care of us when we are weary and overwhelmed, help us and accompany us to Jesus.

Readings from the Fathers of the Church

Saint Ambrose,
If we cannot run, drag us!

How good is the soul that prays not only for itself, but for all! "Drag us," it says. All of us, in fact, have the desire to follow you, a desire inspired by the sweetness of your fragrance. But since we cannot run like you do, drag us, so that with your help and support we may follow in your footsteps. If you drag us, we too will run and will be sped along with spiritual breezes. In fact, the weight is lifted from those who have your hand as support, and upon them is poured the same oil that was used to treat the man wounded by the brigands (cf. Lk 10:30–34).

And lest you think that soul is brazen which says, "Drag us," listen to him who says, "Come to me, all you who are wearied and burdened, and I will refresh you" (cf. Mt 11:28). You see that he drags us willingly, so that we may not remain behind when we follow him.

But he who wants to be dragged, let him run to catch up with him, and let him run, forgetting all the past and desiring the things that are more important. Only in this way, in fact, can he catch up with Christ. Therefore, the apostle also says, "So run that you may obtain it" (cf. 1 Cor 9:24). The soul too desires to arrive at the reward that it longs to obtain.

Reclamation of Our Heart

Fifteenth Sunday of Ordinary Time

✝

Matthew 13:1–23

3 And he spoke to them at length in parables, saying: "A sower went out to sow. 4 And as he sowed, some seed fell on the path, and birds came and ate it up. 5 Some fell on rocky ground, where it had little soil. It sprang up at once because the soil was not deep, 6 and when the sun rose it was scorched, and it withered for lack of roots. 7 Some seed fell among thorns, and the thorns grew up and choked it. 8 But some seed fell on rich soil, and produced fruit, a hundred or sixty or thirtyfold."

When Jesus spoke, he used simple words and he also used images, which were examples taken from daily life, in order to be easily understood by all. This is why they listened to him willingly and appreciated his message, which directly touched their heart. And it was not complicated language as that used by the doctors of the law of that time, which was not easily understood, was very rigid, and distanced people. And with this simple language Jesus made the mystery of the Kingdom of God understood. It was not complicated theology.

One example is that of today's Gospel passage: the parable of the sower (Mt 13:1-23). The sower is Jesus. With this image, we can see that he presents himself as one who does not impose himself, but rather offers himself. He does not attract us by conquering us, but by donating himself: he casts seeds. With patience and generosity, he spreads his Word, which is not a cage or a trap, but a seed which can bear fruit. And how can it bear fruit? If we welcome it.

Therefore, the parable concerns us especially. In fact, it speaks more of the soil than of the sower. Jesus carries out, so to speak, a "spiritual X-ray" of our heart, which is the soil on which the seed of the Word falls. Our heart, like the soil, may be good, and then the Word bears fruit—and a great deal—but it can also be hard and impermeable. This happens when we hear the Word, but it bounces off of us, just as a seed will bounce on a street: it does not enter. If we throw a seed on the *sanpietrini* [cobblestones], nothing grows.

There are, however, two intermediate types of soil which, in different amounts, we can have within us. The first, Jesus says, is *rocky*. Let us try to imagine it: rocky ground is a terrain that "does not have much soil" (v. 13:5), so the seed sprouts but is unable to put down deep roots. This is how the superficial heart is: it welcomes the Lord, wants to pray, love, and bear witness, but does not persevere. It becomes tired and never "takes off." It is a heart without depth, where the rocks of laziness prevail over the good soil, where love is fickle and fleeting. Whoever welcomes the Lord only when they want to does not bear fruit.

Then, there is the last ground, the *thorny* one, filled with briars that choke the good plants. What do these thorns represent? "The cares of the world and the delight in riches" (v. 22), as Jesus says explicitly. The thorns are the vices which come to blows with God, which choke his presence: above all these are the idols of worldly wealth, living avidly, for oneself, for possessions, and for power. If we cultivate these thorns, we choke God's growth within us. Each of us can recognize his or her big or small thorns, the vices that inhabit the heart, those more or less deeply rooted briars that God does not like and that prevent us from having a clean heart. It is necessary to tear them out, otherwise the Word cannot bear fruit and the seed will not grow.

Dear brothers and sisters, Jesus invites us today to look inside ourselves, to give thanks for our good soil and to tend the soil that is not yet good. Let us ask ourselves if our heart is open to welcome the seed of the Word of God with faith. Let us ask ourselves if our rocks of laziness are still numerous and large. Let us identify our thorns of vice and call them by name. Let us find the courage to *reclaim the soil,* to effect a nice conversion of our heart, bringing to the Lord in Confession and in prayer our rocks and our thorns. In doing this, Jesus, the Good Sower, will be glad to carry out an additional task: purifying our hearts by removing the rocks and the thorns that choke his Word.

May the Mother of God, whom we remember today with the title of Blessed Virgin of Mount Carmel, unparalleled in welcoming the Word of God and putting it into practice (cf. Lk 8:21), help us to purify our hearts and welcome the Lord's presence there.

Readings from the Fathers of the Church

Evagrius Ponticus,
Prepare the heart for prayer

Prayer without distraction is the highest activity of the intellect. Prayer is the ascent of the intellect to God. If you desire to pray, renounce everything so that you may inherit everything. Pray, first, to be purified from the passions, then to be freed from ignorance and forgetfulness. And in the third place, pray to be freed from all temptation and dereliction. In your prayers seek only "justice and the kingdom" (Mt 6:33), meaning virtue and knowledge, and all the rest shall be given to you as well.

It is right that one should pray not only for one's own purification, but also for that of one's fellows, for the sake of imitating the behavior of the angels. Take heed that in prayer you are truly in the presence of God, and not, overcome by human praise, driven to go chasing after that praise under the cover of prolonged prayer. Whether you pray with your brothers or alone, strive to pray not out of habit, but with sentiment. The sentiment of prayer consists in a state of the spirit made up of reverence, compunction, and sorrow of the soul in confessing its faults, together with tearful sighing. If your mind distracts itself just when it is time to pray, this means that you do not yet pray like a monk, but are still worldly, busy decorating the outer tent. When you pray, keep watch over your memory, so that this may not fill you with its things, but instead lead you to awareness of the presence.

Imitate God's Patience

Sixteenth Sunday of Ordinary Time

+

Matthew 13:24–43

27 "The slaves of the householder came to him and said, 'Master, did you not sow good seed in your field? Where have the weeds come from?' 28 He answered, 'An enemy has done this.' His slaves said to him, 'Do you want us to go and pull them up?' 29 He replied, 'No, if you pull up the weeds you might uproot the wheat along with them. 30 Let them grow together until harvest; then at harvest time I will say to the harvesters, "First collect the weeds and tie them in bundles for burning; but gather the wheat into my barn."' "

Among Jesus' parables, there is a rather complex one which he explained to the disciples: that of *the good grain and the weeds,* which deals with *the problem of evil* in the world and calls attention to *God's patience* (Mt 13:24–43). The story takes place in a field where the owner sows grain. During the night his enemy comes and sows weeds, a term which in Hebrew derives from the same root as the name Satan, and which alludes to the concept of division. We all know that the demon is a "sower of weeds," one who always seeks to sow division between individuals, families, nations, and peoples. The servants wanted to uproot the weed immediately, but the field owner stopped them, explaining that "in gathering the weeds you root up the wheat along with them" (v. 29). Because we all know that a weed, when it grows, looks very much like good grain, and there is the risk of confusing them.

The teaching of the parable is twofold. First of all, it tells us that the evil in the world *comes not from God but from his enemy, the evil one*. It is curious that the evil one goes at night to sow weeds, in the dark, in confusion; he goes where there is no light to sow weeds. This enemy is astute: he sows evil in the middle of good, thus it is impossible for us men to distinctly separate them; but God, in the end, will be able to do so.

And here we arrive at the second theme: the juxtaposition of the impatience of the servants and the *patient waiting* of the field owner, who represents God. At times we are in a great hurry to judge, to categorize, to put the good here, the bad there. . . . But remember the prayer of that self-righteous man: "God, I thank you that I am not like the rest of humanity— greedy, dishonest, adulterous" (cf. Lk 18:11). God, however, knows how to wait. With patience and mercy he gazes into the "field" of life of every person; he sees the filth and the evil much better than we do, but he also sees the seeds of good, and waits with trust for them to grow. God is patient; he knows how to wait. This is so beautiful: our God is a patient father, who always waits for us and waits with his heart in hand to welcome us, to forgive us. He always forgives us if we go to him.

The field owner's attitude is that of hope grounded in the

certainty that evil has not the first nor the last word. And it is thanks to this *patient hope* of God that the same weed, which is the malicious heart with so many sins, in the end can become good grain. But be careful: evangelical patience is not indifference to evil; one must not confuse good and evil! In facing weeds in the world, the Lord's disciple is called to imitate the patience of God, to nourish hope with the support of indestructible trust in the final victory of good, that is, of God.

In the end, in fact, evil will be removed and eliminated: at the time of harvest, that is, of judgment, the harvesters will follow the orders of the field owner, separating the weed to burn it (cf. Mt 13:30). On the day of the final harvest, *the judge will be Jesus,* he who has sown good grain in the world and who himself became the *"grain of wheat,"* who died and rose. In the end we will all be judged by the same measure with which we have judged: *the mercy we have shown to others will also be shown to us.*

Let us ask Our Lady, our Mother, to help us to grow in patience, in hope, and in mercy with all our brothers and sisters.

Readings from the Fathers of the Church

Tertullian,
Prayer bestows patience

The prayer of old indeed brought freedom from fire (cf. Dn 3:25–50), from beasts (cf. Dn 6:17–24), and from hunger (cf. Dn 14:37), and yet it had not received its content from Christ.

And truly how much more effective is Christian prayer! It does not bring the angel of the dew into the midst of the flames (cf. Dn 3:49–50, 92), it does not seal the mouths of the lions (cf. Dn 6:23), it does not supply the hungry with a rustic meal (cf. Dn 14:33), it does not by any means drive away the experience of passion with a special grace of exemption. It instead brings about the inclination to endurance among those who, while retaining the perception of their sufferings, undergo condemnations. By infusing courage, it brings grace into sharper relief so that believers may know what they obtain from the Lord, being aware of what they undergo for the name of God.

Moreover, the prayer of times past brought about plagues (cf. Ex 7–10), defeated enemy armies (cf. Ex 17:8–15), kept the goodly rain from falling (cf. Dt 11:13–17). Now, the prayer of the just, rather than driving away all of God's wrath, is considerate toward enemies and pleads on behalf of persecutors (cf. Mt 5:44).

The Treasure That Is Jesus
Seventeenth Sunday of Ordinary Time

+

Matthew 13:44–52

44 "The kingdom of heaven is like a treasure buried in a field, which a person finds and hides again, and out of joy goes and sells all that he has and buys that field. 45 Again, the kingdom of heaven is like a merchant searching for fine pearls. 46 When he finds a pearl of great price, he goes and sells all that he has and buys it."

The brief similes proposed in today's liturgy conclude the chapter of the Gospel of Matthew dedicated to the parables of the Kingdom of God (13:44–52). Among these are two small masterpieces: the parable of the treasure hidden in the field and that of the pearl of great value. They tell us that the discovery of the Kingdom of God can happen *suddenly,* like the farmer who, plowing, finds an unexpected treasure; or *after a long search,* like the pearl merchant who eventually finds the most precious pearl, so long dreamed of. Yet, in each case the point is that the treasure and the pearl are worth more than all other possessions. And therefore, when the

farmer and the merchant discover them, they give up everything else in order to obtain them. They do not need to ratio-
nalize or think about it or reflect. They immediately perceive
the incomparable value of what they've found, and they are
prepared to lose everything in order to have it.

This is how it is with the Kingdom of God: those who find
it have no doubts. They sense that this is what they have been
seeking and waiting for; and this is what fulfills their most
authentic aspirations. And it really is like this: those who
know Jesus, encounter him personally, *are captivated, attracted*
by so much goodness, so much truth, so much beauty—and
all with great humility and simplicity. To seek Jesus, to find
Jesus: this is the great treasure!

Many people, many saints, reading the Gospel with an
open heart, have been so struck by Jesus that they convert to
him. Let us think of Saint Francis of Assisi: he was already a
Christian, though a "rosewater" Christian. When he read the
Gospel, in that decisive moment of his youth, he encountered
Jesus and discovered the Kingdom of God. With this, all his
dreams of worldly glory vanished. The Gospel allows you to
know the real Jesus, it lets you know the living Jesus. It speaks
to your heart and changes your life. And then, yes, you leave it
all. You can effectively change lifestyles, or continue to do
what you did before, but *you* are someone else, you are reborn.
You have found what gives meaning, what gives flavor, what
gives light to all things, even to toil, even to suffering, and
even to death.

Read the Gospel. Read the Gospel! We have spoken about
it, do you remember? Read a passage of the Gospel every day.

And carry a little Gospel with us, in our pocket, in a purse, in some way, to keep it at hand. And there, reading a passage, we will find Jesus. Everything takes on meaning when you find your treasure there, in the Gospel. Jesus calls it "the Kingdom of God," that is to say, God who reigns in your life, in our life, God who is love, peace, and joy in every man and in all men. This is what God wants and it is why Jesus gave himself up to death on the Cross, to free us from the power of darkness and to move us into the kingdom of life, of beauty, of goodness, and of joy. To read the Gospel is to find Jesus and to have this Christian joy, which is a gift of the Holy Spirit.

Dear brothers and sisters, the joy of finding the treasure of the Kingdom of God shines through; it's visible. The Christian cannot keep his faith hidden, because it shines through in every word, in every deed, even in the most simple and mundane. The love that God has given through Jesus shines through.

Let us pray, through the intercession of the Virgin Mary, that his Kingdom of love, justice, and peace may reign in us and in the whole world.

Readings from the Fathers of the Church

Saint John Chrysostom,
Christ, treasure of Paul's life

For Paul, there was only one thing to be feared and shunned, and nothing else: offending God. As a result, nothing seemed desirable to him except to please God. And when I say nothing, I do not mean only the goods of this world, but also those of the life to come. I do not speak only of possessions, of peoples, of kingdoms, of armies, of riches, of military honors, of rulership, because in his eyes these treasures were worth less than a wisp of cobweb. I speak also of heavenly goods themselves. Understand this, and you will grasp his ardent love for Christ.

This man, in fact, by virtue of such a love did not allow himself to be attracted by the dignity of the angels, nor by that of the archangels, nor by any such thing. He possessed within himself the richest treasure of all: love for Christ. With this love he deemed himself richer than all men. Without this love, he never would have desired to take part with the heavenly Principalities and Powers; with this love, by contrast, he would have preferred to find himself among the least of men and among the scourged (cf. 2 Cor 6:8–9) rather than, deprived of this love, among the most noble recipients of honors.

Compassionate Eucharist

Eighteenth Sunday of Ordinary Time

✝

Matthew 14:13–21

14 When he disembarked and saw the vast crowd, his heart was moved with pity for them, and he cured their sick. 15 When it was evening, the disciples approached him and said, "This is a deserted place and it is already late; dismiss the crowds so that they can go to the villages and buy food for themselves." 16 [Jesus] said to them, "There is no need for them to go away; give them some food yourselves." 17 But they said to him, "Five loaves and two fish are all we have here." 18 Then he said, "Bring them here to me," 19 and he ordered the crowds to sit down on the grass. Taking the five loaves and the two fish, and looking up to heaven, he said the blessing, broke the loaves, and gave them to the disciples, who in turn gave them to the crowds. 20 They all ate and were satisfied, and they picked up the fragments left over—twelve wicker baskets full.

This Sunday, the Gospel presents to us the miracle of the multiplication of loaves and fish (Mt 14:13–21). Jesus performed it along the Lake of Galilee, in a deserted place where he had withdrawn with his disciples after learning of the death of John the Baptist. But many people followed them and joined them there. Upon seeing them, Jesus felt compassion and healed their sick until the evening. And seeing the late hour, the disciples became concerned and suggested that Jesus send the crowd away so they could go into the villages and buy food to eat. But Jesus calmly replied: "Give them some food yourselves" (v. 16); and he asked them to bring five loaves and two fish, blessed them, began to break the bread and give the food to the disciples, who distributed it to the people. They all ate and were satisfied, and there were even leftovers!

We can understand three messages from this event. The first is *compassion*. In facing the crowd who followed him and, so to speak, "won't leave him alone," Jesus does not react with irritation; he does not say: "These people are bothering me." No, no. He reacts with a feeling of compassion, because he knows they are seeking him not out of curiosity but out of need. But attention: compassion—which Jesus feels—is not simply feeling pity. It's more! It means to *suffer with*, to empathize with the suffering of another, to the point of taking it upon oneself. Jesus is like this: he suffers together with us, he suffers with us, he suffers for us. And the sign of this compassion is the healing he performed on countless people.

Jesus teaches us to place the needs of the poor before our own. Our needs, even if legitimate, are not as urgent as those of the poor, who lack the basic necessities of life. We often speak of the poor. But when we speak of the poor, do we sense that this man or that woman or those children lack the bare

necessities of life? That they have no food, they have no clothing, they cannot afford medicine? Also, that the children do
not have the means to attend school?

The second message is *sharing*. It's helpful to compare the
reaction of the disciples with regard to the tired and hungry
people and that of Jesus. They are different. The disciples
think it would be better to send the crowd away so they can
go and buy food. Jesus instead says: "You give them something to eat." Two different reactions, which reflect two con-
trasting outlooks: the disciples reason with worldly logic, by
which each person must think of himself; they reason as if to
say: "Sort it out for yourselves." Jesus reasons with God's
logic, which is that of sharing. How many times we turn away
so as not to see our brothers in need! And this looking away
is a polite way to say, with white gloves, "Sort it out for yourselves." This is not Jesus' way. This is selfishness. Had he sent
away the crowds, many people would have been left with
nothing to eat. Instead those few loaves and fish, shared and
blessed by God, were enough for everyone. And pay heed! It
isn't magic. It's a "sign": a sign that calls for faith in God,
provident Father, who does not let us go without "our daily
bread," if we know how to share it as brothers.

Compassion, sharing. And the third message: the miracle
of the loaves foreshadows the *Eucharist*. It is seen in the gesture of Jesus, who, before breaking and distributing the
loaves, "blessed" them (v. 19). It is the same gesture that Jesus
was to make at the Last Supper, when he established the per-
petual memorial of his redeeming Sacrifice. In the Eucharist,
Jesus does not give just any bread, but *the* bread of eternal life.

He gives himself, offering himself to the Father out of love for us. But we must go to the Eucharist with those sentiments of Jesus, which are compassion and the will to share. One who goes to the Eucharist without having compassion for the needy and without sharing is not at ease with Jesus.

Compassion, sharing, Eucharist. This is the path that Jesus points out to us in this Gospel, a path which brings us to face the needs of this world with fraternity, but which leads us beyond this world, because it comes from God the Father and returns to him.

May the Virgin Mary, Mother of Divine Providence, accompany us on this journey.

Readings from the Fathers of the Church

Saint John Chrysostom, Eucharist and sharing

Do you want to honor the body of Christ? Do not neglect nakedness; if you honor him with vestments of silk, do not neglect him outside, where he is consumed with cold and nakedness. The same one, in fact, who said: "This is my body" (Mt 26:26) and confirmed the fact with his word, also said: "You saw me hungry and did not feed me" (cf. Mt 25:42). The body of Christ in the Eucharist has no need of vestments, but of a pure soul; the poor man, however, needs a great deal of care. So, let us learn to be wise and to honor Christ as he wishes.

I say this not to hinder those who make such offerings [for

the Church], but because I maintain that it is right that together with these and before these should come almsgiving.
God certainly accepts these as well, but almsgiving much
more. [. . .] What advantage is there if his altar is full of golden
chalices and he is exhausted with hunger? First satisfy his
hunger and then, from what is left over, adorn his table as well.
Do you make a golden chalice and not give a glass of cool
water? And what advantage is there? Do you prepare for the
table vestments embroidered with gold, and do not even offer
to him the necessary clothing? And what profit do you get
from this?

In the Church Boat

Nineteenth Sunday of Ordinary Time

✝

Matthew 14:22–33

26 When the disciples saw him walking on the sea they were terrified. "It is a ghost," they said, and they cried out in fear. 27 At once [Jesus] spoke to them, "Take courage, it is I; do not be afraid." 28 Peter said to him in reply, "Lord, if it is you, command me to come to you on the water." 29 He said, "Come." Peter got out of the boat and began to walk on the water toward Jesus. 30 But when he saw how [strong] the wind was he became frightened; and, beginning to sink, he cried out, "Lord, save me!" 31 Immediately Jesus stretched out his hand and caught him, and said to him, "O you of little faith, why did you doubt?" 32 After they got into the boat, the wind died down. 33 Those who were in the boat did him homage, saying, "Truly, you are the Son of God."

Today the Gospel passage describes the episode about Jesus who, after praying all night on the shore of the Lake of Galilee, makes his way toward his disciples' boat, walking on the water. The boat is in the middle of the lake, halted by a strong wind blowing against it. When they see Jesus come walking on the water, the disciples mistake him for a ghost, and they are afraid. But he reassures them: "Take courage, it is I; do not be afraid" (Mt 14:27). Peter, with his characteristic impetuousness, says to him: "Lord, if it is you, command me to come to you on the water." And Jesus calls him: "Come!" (vv. 28–29). Peter gets out of the boat and begins to walk on the water toward Jesus; but because of the wind, he is afraid and starts to sink. So he cries out: "Lord, save me!" And Jesus reaches out his hand and catches him (vv. 30–31).

This Gospel narrative contains rich symbolism, and makes us reflect on our faith, both as individuals and as an ecclesial community. It also causes us to reflect on the faith of all of us who are here today in the square. Does the community, this ecclesial community, have faith? How is the faith in each of us, and the faith of our community? The boat is the life of each one of us, but it is also the life of the Church. The wind against it represents difficulties and trials. Peter's invocation— "Lord, command me to come to you!"—and his cry—"Lord, save me!"—are very similar to our desire to feel the Lord's closeness, but also express the real fear and anguish that accompany the most difficult moments of our life and of our communities, marked by internal fragility and external difficulties.

At that moment, Jesus' word of reassurance, which was like an outstretched rope to cling to in the face of the hostile and turbulent waters, was not enough for Peter. This is what can happen to us as well. When one does not cling to the

Word of the Lord to feel secure, but consults horoscopes and fortune-tellers, one begins to sink. This means that the faith is not very strong. Today's Gospel reminds us that faith in the Lord and in his Word does not open a way for us where everything is easy and calm; it does not rescue us from life's storms. Faith gives us the assurance of a presence, the presence of Jesus, who encourages us to overcome the existential tempests, the certainty of a hand that grabs hold of us so as to help us face the difficulties, pointing the way for us even when it is dark. Faith, in short, is not an escape route from life's problems, but it sustains the journey and gives it meaning.

This episode offers a wonderful image of the reality of the Church throughout the ages: a boat that, as she makes the crossing, must also weather contrary winds and storms, which threaten to capsize her. What save her are not the courage and qualities of her men. The guarantee against shipwreck is faith in Christ and in his Word. This is the guarantee: faith in Jesus and in his Word. We are safe on this boat, despite our wretchedness and weaknesses, especially when we are kneeling and worshiping the Lord, like the disciples who, in the end, fell down before him, saying, "Truly, you are the Son of God!" (v. 33). How beautiful it is to say this to Jesus: "Truly you are the Son of God!" Shall we say it together, all of us? "Truly you are the Son of God!"

May the Virgin Mary help us to remain steadfast in the faith, to resist life's tempests, to remain on the barque of the Church by shunning the temptation to embark on the se-

ductive but insecure boats of ideologies, fashions, and slo-gans.

Readings from the Fathers of the Church

Saint Ambrose,
The barque of Peter

This barque, which carries Peter, does not let itself be shaken. The one that is shaken is instead that which carries Judas. Even if all the merits of the apostles were to sail on that ship, nonetheless it would still be jolted by the traitor's betrayal. Peter is in both, but although he is safe on account of his own actions, he is shaken on account of those of others. Let us guard ourselves against the betrayer, let us guard ourselves against the traitor, that many may not be tossed about because of just one.

But this ship, on which prudence sails, is not shaken, disbelief is kept far away and it is blown by the breeze of faith. And how could it waver if it is steered by the one who is the foundation of the Church? The storm breaks only where there is little faith.

And where there is perfect love, safety is found. Besides, although the other apostles receive the order to cast the nets, only Peter is told: "Cast out into the deep" (Lk 5:4), that is, steer into the profundities of the disputes. What is there that is more immense than seeing the depth of the riches, knowing the Son of God, and daring to profess his divine generation? And although the human intellect cannot understand it, in spite of investigating it with all the powers of reason, nonetheless the fullness of faith can embrace it. [. . .]

It is toward these theological depths that Peter steers the Church, so that it may see on one side the Resurrection of the Son, and on the other the outpouring of the Holy Spirit.

The Power of Humility

The Assumption of the Blessed Virgin Mary

+

Luke 1:39–56

39 During those days Mary set out and traveled to the hill country in haste to a town of Judah, 40 where she entered the house of Zechariah and greeted Elizabeth. 41 When Elizabeth heard Mary's greeting, the infant leaped in her womb, and Elizabeth, filled with the holy Spirit, 42 cried out in a loud voice and said, "Most blessed are you among women, and blessed is the fruit of your womb. 43 And how does this happen to me, that the mother of my Lord should come to me? 44 For at the moment the sound of your greeting reached my ears, the infant in my womb leaped for joy. 45 Blessed are you who believed that what was spoken to you by the Lord would be fulfilled." 46 And Mary said: "My soul proclaims the greatness of the Lord."

Today, the Solemnity of the Assumption of the Blessed Virgin Mary, the Gospel introduces us to the young woman of Nazareth who, having received the Angel's Annunciation, leaves in haste to be closer to Elizabeth in the final months of her prodigious pregnancy. Arriving at Elizabeth's home, Mary hears her utter the words that have come to form the Hail Mary prayer: "Most blessed are you among women, and blessed is the fruit of your womb" (Lk 1:42). In fact, the greatest gift Mary brings to Elizabeth—and to the whole world—is Jesus, who already lives within her; and he lives not only through faith and through expectation, as in many women of the Old Testament: from the Virgin, Jesus took on human flesh for his mission of salvation.

In the home of Elizabeth and her husband, Zechariah, where sadness once reigned for lack of children, there is now the joy of a child on the way: a child who will become the great John the Baptist, the precursor of the Messiah. And when Mary arrives, joy overflows and gushes from their hearts, because the invisible but real presence of Jesus fills everything with meaning: life, family, the salvation of the people. Everything! This joy is expressed in Mary's voice in the marvelous prayer that the Gospel of Luke has conveyed to us and that, from the first Latin word, is called *Magnificat*. It is a song of praise to God, who works great things through humble people, unknown to the world, as is Mary herself; as is her spouse, Joseph; and as is the place where they live, Nazareth. The great things God has done with humble people, the great things the Lord does in the world with the humble, because humility is like a vacuum that leaves room for God. The humble are powerful because they are humble, not because they are strong. And this is the greatness of the humble and of humility. I would like to ask you and also myself—but do not answer out loud—each of you respond in your heart: How is my humility?

The *Magnificat* praises the merciful and faithful God, who accomplishes his plan of salvation through the little ones and the poor, through those who have faith in him, who trust in his Word as did Mary. Here is the exclamation of Elizabeth: "Blessed are you who believed" (v. 45). In that house, the coming of Jesus through Mary created not only a climate of joy and fraternal communion but also a climate of faith that leads to hope, prayer, and praise.

We would like to have all of this happen today in our homes too. Celebrating Mary Most Holy Assumed into Heaven, we would once again wish her to bring to us, to our families, to our communities, this immense gift, that unique grace that we must always seek first and above all the other graces that we also have at heart: the grace that is Jesus Christ!

By bearing Jesus, Our Lady also brings to us a new joy full of meaning; she brings us a new ability to traverse with faith the most painful and difficult moments; she brings us the capacity of mercy, in order to forgive each other, to understand each other, and to support each other.

Mary is the model of virtue and of faith. Today, in contemplating her Assumption into Heaven, the final fulfillment of her earthly journey, we thank her because she always precedes us in the pilgrimage of life and faith. She is the first disciple. And we ask her to keep us and support us, that we may have a strong, joyful, and merciful faith, and that she may help us to be saints, to meet with her, one day, in heaven.

Readings from the Fathers of the Church

Saint Ambrose,
The humility of Mary

Mary says: "Behold the handmaid of the Lord; be it done unto me according to your word" (Lk 1:38). What humility, what devotion! While she is chosen as mother, she professes herself handmaid of the Lord, and does not get carried away by the sudden promise. Likewise, in calling herself handmaid, she did not lay claim to any of the privileges that indeed came to her from such a great gift, but simply wanted to do what was required of her. And since she was to bring forth him who is meek and humble, she too had to give proof of her humility. "Behold the handmaid of the Lord; be it done unto me according to your word." Behold her obedience, behold her desire. In fact, the words "Behold the handmaid of the Lord" signify that she is ready to serve. "Be it done unto me according to your word" expresses that the desire has been realized.

With what promptness, then, did Mary believe, in spite of finding herself in such an exceptional condition! [. . .] It comes as no surprise that the Lord, having to redeem the world, should have begun his work with Mary. If it was through her that salvation was being prepared for all men, she should have been the first to obtain from her Son the fruit of salvation.

The Courage of Prayer
Twentieth Sunday of Ordinary Time

✝

Matthew 15:21–28

25 But the woman came and did him homage, saying, "Lord, help me." 26 He said in reply, "It is not right to take the food of the children and throw it to the dogs." 27 She said, "Please, Lord, for even the dogs eat the scraps that fall from the table of their masters." 28 Then Jesus said to her in reply, "O woman, great is your faith! Let it be done for you as you wish." And her daughter was healed from that hour.

Today's Gospel presents to us a unique example of faith in Jesus' encounter with a Canaanite woman, a foreigner to the Jews. The scene unfolds as he is walking toward the cities of Tyre and Sidon, northwest of Galilee: it is here that the woman begs Jesus to heal her daughter, who, the Gospel says, "is severely possessed by a demon" (Mt 15:22). The Lord, at first, seems not to hear this cry of pain, prompting the disciples to intercede for her. Jesus' seeming indifference does not discourage this mother, who persists in her invocation.

This woman's inner strength, which enables her to overcome every obstacle, is to be found in her *maternal love* and in her *faith* that Jesus can grant her request. This makes me think of the strength of women. With their strength they are able to obtain great things. We have known many [such women]! We could say that it is love that stirs faith, and faith, for its part, becomes love's reward. Heartrending love for her daughter causes the woman to cry: "Have mercy on me, Lord, Son of David" (v. 22). And her untiring faith in Jesus allows her not to become discouraged even in the face of his initial rejection; thus, the woman knelt before him, saying, "Lord, help me" (v. 25).

In the end, before such persistence, Jesus was in awe, nearly astonished, by the faith of a pagan woman. It causes him to acquiesce, saying: "'O woman, great is your faith! Let it be done for you as you wish.' And her daughter was healed from that hour" (v. 28). Jesus points to this humble woman as a model of unwavering faith. Her persistence in beseeching Christ's intervention is incentive for us not to become discouraged, not to despair when we are burdened by life's difficult trials. The Lord does not turn away in the face of our needs and, if at times he seems insensitive to our requests for help, it is in order to put to the test and to strengthen our faith. We must continue to cry out like this woman: "Lord, help me! Lord, help me!" We must cry out in this way, with perseverance and courage. This is the courage needed in prayer.

This Gospel episode helps us to understand that we all need to grow in faith and fortify our trust in Jesus. He can help us find our way when we have lost the compass of our journey, when the road no longer seems flat but rough and arduous, when it is hard to be faithful to our commitments. It is important to nourish our faith every day, by carefully listening to the Word of God, with the celebration of the Sacraments, with personal prayer as a "cry" to him—"Lord, help me!"—and with concrete acts of charity toward our neighbor.

Let us entrust ourselves to the Holy Spirit, so that he may help us to persevere in faith. The Spirit instills courage in the hearts of believers; he gives our life and our Christian witness the power of conviction and persuasion; he helps us to overcome skepticism toward God and indifference toward our brothers and sisters.

May the Virgin Mary render us ever more aware of our need of the Lord and of his Spirit; may she obtain for us a strong faith, full of love, and a love capable of making itself a supplication, a courageous supplication to God.

Readings from the Fathers of the Church

Saint Basil the Great, The courage given by the Holy Spirit

The Lord, preparing us for the life that is unleashed by the redemption, sets before us the whole code of conduct of the Gospels, directing us not to become angry, to be meek, to remain pure from the love of pleasure, to conduct ourselves with detachment from money, so that by our deliberate choice we may remain on the right path, employing ourselves even now in that which is the proper and natural possession of eternal life. [. . .]

The work of the Holy Spirit brings about our restitution to paradise, our ascent to the Kingdom of Heaven, the return of filial adoption, the freedom to call God our Father, communion in the grace of Christ, being called children of the light, participation in eternal glory, and in a word, being in the fullness of blessing, during this life and in the future, contemplating as in a mirror the gift of the benefits that are reserved for us in the promises already present, the fruition of which we await through faith.

A Heart as Firm as Stone

Twenty-First Sunday of Ordinary Time

✝

Matthew 16:13–20

15 He said to them, "But who do you say that I am?" 16 Simon Peter said in reply, "You are the Messiah, the Son of the living God." 17 Jesus said to him in reply, "Blessed are you, Simon son of Jonah. For flesh and blood has not revealed this to you, but my heavenly Father. 18 And so I say to you, you are Peter, and upon this rock I will build my church, and the gates of the netherworld shall not prevail against it."

This Sunday's Gospel reading (Mt 16:13–20) is a well-known passage, central to Matthew's account, in which Simon, on behalf of the twelve, professes his faith in Jesus as "the Christ, the Son of the living God" (v. 16); and Jesus calls Simon "blessed" for this faith, recognizing in him a special gift of the Father, and tells him: "You are Peter, and upon this rock I will build my church"(v. 18).

Let us pause on this very point, on the fact that Jesus gives

Simon this name, Peter, which in Jesus' language is pronounced "Kefa," a word which means "rock." In the Bible this term, "rock," refers to God. Jesus gives it to Simon not because of his character or for his merits as a human, but for his *genuine and steadfast faith*, which comes to him from above.

Jesus feels great joy in his heart because, in Simon, he recognizes the hand of the Father, the work of the Holy Spirit. He recognizes that God the Father has given Simon "steadfast" faith on which he, Jesus, can build his Church, meaning his community—all of us. Jesus intends to give life to "his" Church, a people founded no longer on heritage, but on *faith*, which means on the relationship with him, a relationship of love and trust. The Church is built on our relationship with Jesus. And to begin his Church, Jesus needs to find solid faith, "steadfast" faith in his disciples. And it is this that he must verify at this point of the journey.

The Lord has in mind a picture of the structure, an image of the community like a building. This is why, when he hears Simon's candid profession of faith, he calls him a "rock" and declares his intention to build his Church upon this faith.

Brothers and sisters, what happened in a unique way in Saint Peter also happens in every Christian who develops a sincere faith in Jesus the Christ, the Son of the Living God. Today's Gospel passage also asks each of us, "Is your faith good?" Each one answer in his or her heart: Is my faith good? How does the Lord find my heart? Does he find a heart that is firm as a rock, or a heart like sand, that is doubtful, diffident, disbelieving? It will do us good to think about this throughout the day today. If the Lord finds in our heart—I don't say a perfect but—a sincere, genuine faith, then he also sees in us living stones with which to build his community. This community's foundation stone is Christ, the unique cornerstone. On his side, Peter is the rock, the visible foundation of the Church's unity; and every baptized person is called to offer Jesus his or her lowly but sincere faith, so that he may continue to build his Church today, in every part of the world.

Even today, so many people think Jesus may be a great prophet, a knowledgeable teacher, a model of justice. [. . .] And even today Jesus asks his disciples, that is, all of us: "Who do you say that I am?" What do we answer? Let us think about this. But above all, let us pray to God the Father, through the intercession of the Virgin Mary; let us pray that he grant us the grace to respond, with a sincere heart: "You are the Christ, the Son of the living God." This is a confession of faith, this is really "the Creed."

Let us entrust ourselves to Mary, Queen of the Apostles, Mother of the Church. She was in the Upper Room next to Peter when the Holy Spirit descended upon the apostles and spurred them to go out to proclaim to all that Jesus is Lord. Today may our Mother sustain us and accompany us through her intercession, so that we may fully realize that unity and that communion for which Christ and the apostles prayed and gave their lives.

Readings from the Fathers of the Church

Saint Ambrose,
Strive, that you too may be a rock

Christ is the rock—"all," in fact, "drank from one rock that accompanied them, and that rock was Christ" (1 Cor 10:4)—but he did not withhold this excellent name from his disciple, in such a way that he too might be Peter, receiving from the rock firmness of perseverance and unshakable faith.

Strive that you too may be a rock. But for this do not seek outside yourself, but inside yourself for the rock. Your rock is your actions, your rock is your thought. On this rock your house is built, so that it may not be battered by any storm of the spirits of evil. Your rock is faith, because faith is the foundation of the Church. If you are a rock, you will be inside the Church, because the Church stands on the rock. If you are inside the Church, the gates of Hades will not prevail against you. The gates of Hades are the gates of death, but the gates of death cannot be the gates of the Church.

There Is No True Love Without Sacrifice

Twenty-Second Sunday of Ordinary Time

✝

Matthew 16:21–27

21 From that time on, Jesus began to show his disciples that he must go to Jerusalem and suffer greatly from the elders, the chief priests, and the scribes, and be killed and on the third day be raised. 22 Then Peter took him aside and began to rebuke him, "God forbid, Lord! No such thing shall ever happen to you." 23 He turned and said to Peter, "Get behind me, Satan! You are an obstacle to me. You are thinking not as God does, but as human beings do."

Today's Gospel passage (Mt 16:21–27) is the continuation of last Sunday's, which highlighted the profession of faith of Peter, the "rock" upon which Jesus wishes to build his Church. Today, in stark contrast, Matthew shows us the reaction of the same Peter when Jesus reveals to his disciples that he will have to suffer, be killed, and rise again (cf. v. 21). Peter takes the Teacher aside and reproaches him because this, he says, cannot happen to him, to Christ. But Jesus, in turn, rebukes Peter with harsh words: "Get behind me, Satan! You are an obstacle to me. You are thinking not as God does, but as human beings do" (v. 23). A moment before, the apostle had been blessed by the Father, because he had received that revelation from him; he was a solid "rock" so that Jesus could build his community upon him; and immediately afterward he becomes an obstacle, a rock, but not for building, a stumbling block on the Messiah's path. Jesus knows well that Peter and the others still have a long way to go to become his apostles!

At that point, the Teacher turns to all those who were following him, clearly presenting to them the path to follow: "Whoever wishes to come after me must deny himself, take up his cross, and follow me" (v. 24). Always, today too, the temptation is that of wanting to follow a Christ without the cross, and, on the contrary, to teach God which is the right path, like Peter, saying, "No, no, Lord! This shall never happen." But Jesus reminds us that his way is the way of love, and that there is no true love without self-sacrifice. We are called to not let ourselves be absorbed by the vision of this world, but to be ever more aware of the need and of the effort for us Christians to walk against the current and uphill.

Jesus completes his proposal with words that express a great and ever valid wisdom, because they challenge the egocentric mentality and behavior. He exhorts: "For whoever wishes to save his life will lose it, but whoever loses his life for my sake will find it" (v. 25). This paradox contains the golden rule that God inscribed in human nature created in Christ: the rule that only love gives meaning and happiness to life. To spend one's own talents, one's energy, and one's time only to save, protect, and fulfill oneself in reality leads to losing oneself, that is, to a sad and barren existence. Instead, let us live for the Lord and base our life on love, as Jesus did: we will be able to savor authentic joy, and our life will not be barren; it will be fruitful.

In the Eucharistic celebration we relive the mystery of the Cross; we not only remember, but we commemorate the redeeming Sacrifice in which the Son of God completely loses himself so as to be received anew by the Father and thus find us again, we who were lost, together with all creatures. Each time we take part in the Holy Mass, the love of the crucified and Risen Christ is conveyed to us as food and drink, so that we may follow him on the daily path, in concrete service to our brothers and sisters.

> May Mary Most Holy, who followed Jesus up to Calvary, accompany us too and help us not to be afraid of the cross, but with Jesus nailed [to it], not a cross without Jesus, the Cross with Jesus, which is the cross of suffering for love of God and of our brothers and sisters, because this suffering, by the grace of Christ, bears the fruit of resurrection.

Readings from the Fathers of the Church

Saint Augustine,
The true sacrifice

True sacrifice is every work with which we seek to unite ourselves in holy communion to God, in such a way that [this work] may be ascribed to the ultimate good by which we can be truly happy. Therefore, even the good of bringing aid to man, if it is not performed in relation to God, is not sacrifice. In fact, although sacrifice is performed and offered by man, it is a divine thing; so much so that even the old Latins called it this. Therefore, the man who is consecrated in the name of God and promised to him, in that he dies to the world in order to live for God, is himself a sacrifice.

[. . .] Now the true sacrifices are the works of mercy for ourselves and for our neighbor, when they are ascribed to God. The works of mercy, furthermore, are performed in order to be freed from unhappiness and become happy; and this is obtained only with that good of which it has been said: "My good is to unite myself to God" (Ps 73:28). [. . .] The apostle has therefore exhorted us to present our bodies as a living offering, holy and pleasing to God, as our rational worship, not to conform ourselves to the world that passes but to reform ourselves in the renewal of conscience, that we may become aware of what is the will of God, the action that is good, pleasing, and perfect. [. . .] This is the sacrifice of Christians: many, and "one body" (1 Cor 12:13) in Christ. The Church celebrates this mystery with the sacrament of the altar, known to the faithful, in which it is revealed to her that in the thing she offers she herself is offered.

Brotherly Correction

Twenty-Third Sunday of Ordinary Time

✝

Matthew 18:15–20

15 "If your brother sins [against you], go and tell him his fault between you and him alone. If he listens to you, you have won over your brother. 16 If he does not listen, take one or two others along with you, so that 'every fact may be established on the testimony of two or three witnesses.' 17 If he refuses to listen to them, tell the church. If he refuses to listen even to the church, then treat him as you would a Gentile or a tax collector."

The Gospel this Sunday (Mt 18:15–20) presents the theme of brotherly correction within the community of believers: that is, how must I correct another Christian when he does what is not good? Jesus teaches us that, should my Christian brother commit a sin against me, offend me, I must be charitable toward him and, first of all, speak with him personally, and explain to him what he said or did that was wrong. What if the brother doesn't listen to me? Jesus proposes a progressive intervention: first, return and speak to him with two or three other people, so he may be more aware of his error; if, despite this, he does not accept the admonition, the community must be told. Should he also refuse to listen to the community, he must be made aware of the rift and estrangement that he himself has caused, weakening the communion with his brothers in the faith.

The stages of this plan show the effort that the Lord asks of his community in order to accompany the one who transgresses, so that he or she is not lost. It is important above all to prevent any clamor in the news and gossip in the community—this is the first thing, and must be avoided. "Go and tell him his fault between you and him alone" (v. 15). The approach is one of sensitivity, prudence, humility, attention toward the one who committed a fault, in order to avoid wounding or killing the brother with words. Because, you know, words too can kill! When I speak, when I make an unfair criticism, when I "flay" a brother with my tongue, this is killing another person's reputation! Words kill too. Let us pay attention to this. At the same time, the discretion of speaking to him alone is to avoid needlessly humiliating the sinner. It is discussed between the two; no one is aware of it and then it's over.

This requirement also takes into account the consequent series of interventions calling for the involvement of a few witnesses and then actually of the community. The purpose is to help the person realize what he has done, and that through his fault he has offended not only one, but everyone. But it also helps us to free ourselves from anger or resentment, which only causes harm: that bitterness of heart which brings anger and resentment, and which leads us to insult and aggression. It's terrible to see an insult or taunt issue from the mouth of a Christian. It is ugly. Do you understand? Do not insult! To insult is not Christian. Understood? To insult is not Christian.

Actually, before God we are all sinners and in need of forgiveness. All of us. Indeed, Jesus told us not to judge. Fraternal correction is a mark of the love and communion that must reign in the Christian community. It is, rather, a mutual service that we can and must render to one another. To reprove a brother is a service, and it is possible and effective only if each one recognizes himself to be a sinner and in need of the Lord's forgiveness. The same awareness that enables me to recognize the fault of another, even before that, reminds me that I have likewise made mistakes and I am often wrong.

This is why, at the beginning of Mass, every time, we are called before the Lord to recognize that we are sinners, expressing through words and gestures sincere repentance of the heart. And we say: "Have mercy on me, Lord. I am a sinner! I confess to Almighty God my sins." We don't say: "Lord, have mercy on this man who is beside me, or this woman, who are sinners." No! "Have mercy on me!" we say. We are all sinners and in need of the Lord's forgiveness. It is the Holy Spirit who speaks to our spirit and makes us recognize our faults in light of the Word of Jesus. And Jesus himself invites us all, saints and sinners, to his table, gathering us from the crossroads, from diverse situations of life (cf. Mt 22:9-10).

And two conditions held in common among those participating in the Eucharistic celebration are fundamental in order to go to Mass correctly: we are all sinners, and God grants his mercy to all. These are the two conditions which open wide the doors that we might enter Mass properly. We must always remember this before addressing a brother in brotherly correction.

Readings from the Fathers of the Church

Saint Augustine, Charity is fervent in correcting

If you want to preserve charity, brothers, above all do not think that it is demeaning and tedious; do not think that it is preserved by virtue of a certain softness, even by passivity and negligence. This is not how it is preserved. So do not believe that you love your servant because you do not beat him; or that you love your child because you do not punish him; or that you love your neighbor when you do not reprimand him. This is not charity, but disregard. Let charity be fervent in correcting, in amending. If the customs are good, you should be happy about this; if they are bad, they should be amended, and they should be corrected. Do not wish to love the error in man, but man. God in fact made man; man, however, made error. Love that which God made. Do not love what man himself made. Loving this means destroying that: when you love the one you correct the other. Even if at times you appear to be cruel, let this come about through the desire to correct.

This is why charity is symbolized by the dove placed above the Lord (cf. Mt 3:16), that form of the dove, in which the Holy Spirit came to infuse charity into us. [. . .]

A father does this as well when he punishes his child: he punishes him to correct him. As I have said, the merchant, in order to make a sale, uses flattery but is hard at heart: the father in correcting punishes, but is without hostility. So should you too be toward all.

A Mercy Without Limits
Twenty-Fourth Sunday of Ordinary Time

✝

Matthew 18:21–35

21 Then Peter approaching asked him, "Lord, if my brother sins against me, how often must I forgive him? As many as seven times?" 22 Jesus answered, "I say to you, not seven times but seventy-seven times."

This Sunday's Gospel passage (Mt 18:21–35) offers us a lesson on forgiveness which does not deny wrongdoing, but recognizes that human beings, created in God's image, are always greater than the evil they commit. Saint Peter asks Jesus: "Lord, if my brother sins against me, how often must I forgive him? As many as seven times?" (v. 21). To Peter, forgiving the same person seven times already seemed the maximum possible. And perhaps to us it already seems too much to do so twice. But Jesus answers, "I say to you, not seven times but seventy-seven times" (v. 22), meaning *always*. You must always forgive. And he confirms this by telling the parable of the merciful king and the wicked servant, in which he shows the inconsistency of the man who was first forgiven and then refused to forgive.

The king in the parable is a generous man who, spurred by compassion, forgives an enormous debt—"10,000 talents" of a servant who beseeches him. That same servant, however, as soon as he meets another servant like himself who owes him 100 denarii—a much smaller amount—behaves in a ruthless way and has him thrown in prison. The servant's inconsistent behavior is the same as ours when we refuse to forgive our brothers and sisters. Whereas the king in the parable is the image of God, who loves us with a love that is so rich in mercy as to welcome us, love us, and forgive us continuously.

From the time of our Baptism, God has forgiven us, releasing us from an intractable debt: original sin. But that is the first time. Then, with boundless mercy, he forgives us all our faults as soon as we show even the least sign of repentance. This is how God is: merciful. When we are tempted to close our heart to those who have offended us and tell us they are sorry, let us remember our Heavenly Father's words to the wicked servant: "I forgave you your entire debt because you begged me to. Should you not have had pity on your fellow servant, as I had pity on you?" (vv. 32–33). Anyone who has experienced the joy, peace, and inner freedom that come from being forgiven should open himself or herself up to the possibility of forgiving in turn.

Jesus wished to introduce the teaching of this parable into the Our Father. He linked the forgiveness that we ask from God with the forgiveness that we should accord our brothers and sisters: "And forgive us our debts, as we also have forgiven our debtors" (Mt 6:12). God's forgiveness is the symbol of his "overflowing" love for each of us. It is the love that leaves us free to distance ourselves, like the prodigal son, but that awaits our return every day. It is the resourceful love of the Shepherd for the lost sheep. It is the tenderness that welcomes each sinner who knocks at his door. The Heavenly Father—our Father—is filled, is full of love, and he wants to offer it to us. But he cannot do so if we close our heart to love toward others.

May the Virgin Mary help us to become ever more aware of the gratuitousness and the greatness of the forgiveness received from God, to become merciful like him, Good Father, slow to anger and great in love.

Readings from the Fathers of the Church

Saint Polycarp, Forgiving our brother

Let the presbyters also be compassionate, merciful toward all, bring the straying back to the right way, visit all the sick, not neglect the widow, orphan, or poor, concern themselves always with what is admirable before God and men, abstain entirely from anger, from partiality, from unjust judgment, keep themselves far from greed, not be quick to believe evil of others, not be rigid in judgment, knowing that we are all debtors in sin.

So if we pray to the Lord to forgive us, we should also forgive: because we are before the eyes of the Lord and God, and we must all present ourselves before the tribunal of Christ and render an account of ourselves. So let us serve him in this way, with fear and reverence, as he himself has commanded, as well as the apostles who preached the Gospel to us and the prophets who foretold the coming of our Lord. Let us be zealous in the good, keeping ourselves far from scandals, from false brothers, and from those who bear the name of the Lord with hypocrisy and deceive men of no account.

God Does Not Exclude Anyone

Twenty-Fifth Sunday of Ordinary Time

✝

Matthew 20:1–16

13 "He said to one of them in reply, 'My friend, I am not cheating you. Did you not agree with me for the usual daily wage? 14 Take what is yours and go. What if I wish to give this last one the same as you? 15 [Or] am I not free to do as I wish with my own money? Are you envious because I am generous?' 16 Thus, the last will be first, and the first will be last."

In today's Gospel reading (Mt 20:1–16) there is the parable of the day laborers in the vineyard, which Jesus recounts in order to explain two aspects of the Kingdom of God: the first is that God wants to call everyone to work for his Kingdom; the second is that, in the end, he wants to give everyone the same reward, that is, salvation, eternal life.

The owner of the vineyard, who represents God, goes out at dawn and hires a group of workers, agreeing with them on the day's wages. It was a fair wage. Then he goes out again later in the day—he goes out five times on that day—until the late afternoon to hire other unemployed laborers whom he sees. At the end of the day, the landowner orders that a denarius be paid to everyone, even to those who had worked for only a few hours. Naturally, the laborers who were hired first complain, because they see that they are paid as much as those who worked for fewer hours. The landowner, however, reminds them about what had been agreed; if he then wants to be generous with the others, they should not be envious.

In reality, this "injustice" of the owner serves to provoke in those listening to the parable a qualitative leap, because here Jesus does not want to speak about the issue of work or of a fair wage, but about the Kingdom of God! And this is the message: There are no unemployed people in the Kingdom of God. Everyone is called to do their part. And there will be a reward from divine justice for everyone in the end—not from human [justice], luckily!—but the salvation that Jesus Christ acquired for us with his death and Resurrection. This is a salvation that is not deserved, but donated—salvation is free— thus, "the last will be the first and the first last" (v. 16).

With this parable, Jesus wants to open our hearts to the logic of the Father's love, which is free and generous. It is about allowing oneself to be astonished and fascinated by the "thoughts" and the "ways" of God, which, as the prophet Isaiah recalls, are not our thoughts and not our ways (cf. Is 55:8). Human thoughts are often marked by selfishness and personal advantage, and our narrow and contorted paths are not comparable to the wide and straight streets of the Lord. He uses mercy—do not forget this: he uses mercy—he forgives broadly, and is filled with generosity and kindness, which he pours forth on each of us. He opens for everyone the bound-less territory of his love and his grace, which alone can give the human heart the fullness of joy.

Jesus wants to make us contemplate the gaze of that land-owner, the gaze with which he looks upon each of the labor-ers searching for work and calls them to go to his vineyard. It is a gaze filled with attention, kindness. It is a gaze which calls, invites one to get up and begin a journey, because he wants life for each of us. He wants a full, committed life, safe from emptiness and inertia. God excludes no one and wants each of us to achieve his or her fullness. This is the love of our God, of our God who is Father.

May Mary Most Holy help us welcome into our lives the logic of love, which frees us from the presumption of de-serving God's reward and from the critical judgment of others.

Readings from the Fathers of the Church

Saint Gregory the Great,
Do not be jealous of the gifts received

It is good when humility is accompanied by consideration, and consideration by the interior unity of the spirit.

There are, in fact, some who receive great gifts of virtue and stand out through their lofty qualities in leading others: they are pure through their commitment to chastity, solid through their seriousness in mortification, equipped with treasures of doctrine, humble through generosity of patience, dignified by virtue of authority, gentle by virtue of compassion, rigorous in the severity of justice. These, if they refuse the great responsibilities for souls in the ministry, even when they are called to it, often end up finding themselves deprived of the gifts that they received not only for themselves, but also for others. Attentive to their own advantages and not to those of their neighbor, they deprive themselves of the gifts that they would like to enjoy exclusively. [. . .]

Anyone who has the talents but refuses to feed God's flock shows by this that he does not love the supreme Shepherd. For this reason, Paul says: "If Christ died for all, then all have died. He died for all, that those who live may no longer live for themselves, but for him who died and rose for them" (cf. 2 Cor 5:14–15).

A Poor, Humble Church That Trusts in the Lord

Twenty-Sixth Sunday of Ordinary Time

✝

Matthew 21:28–32

31 "Amen, I say to you, tax collectors and prostitutes are entering the kingdom of God before you. 32 When John came to you in the way of righteousness, you did not believe him; but tax collectors and prostitutes did. Yet even when you saw that, you did not later change your minds and believe him."

In today's passage from the Gospel according to Matthew (21:28–32), Jesus states to the chief priests and elders: "Amen, I say to you, tax collectors and prostitutes are entering the kingdom of God before you" (v. 31). Jesus speaks clearly here, with the courage to tell the truth even with those who were considered masters in the way of thinking, judging, and acting.

The question then arises: What should the Church be like? The people we read about in the Bible were indeed men of the Church. They were heads of the Church. Jesus came, John the

Baptist came, but those men didn't listen. In the passage from the Book of Zephaniah, the prophet recalls that although God chose his people, this people became a rebellious city, an impure city. They did not accept how the Church should be, how the People of God should be.

However, Zephaniah communicates God's promise to the people: "I will forgive you" (Zep 3:15). That is, in order for the People of God, the Church, all of us to be faithful, the first step is to feel we are forgiven.

After the promise of forgiveness, there is also the explanation of how the Church is supposed to be: "But I will leave as a remnant in your midst a people humble and lowly, who shall take refuge in the name of the Lord" (Zep 3:12). Thus, the faithful People of God must have these three traits: humble, lowly, with trust in the Lord.

First of all, the Church has to be humble. In other words, a Church should not show off her powers, her grandeur. However, humility doesn't mean a lethargic, weary person with a demure expression, because this is not humility, this is theatrics! This is feigned humility. True humility, instead, begins with the first step: "I am a sinner." If you are not able to tell yourself that you are a sinner and that others are better than you, you are not humble. Thus, the first step for a humble Church is feeling that she is a sinner, and the same is true for all of us. On the other hand, if any of us has the habit of looking at others' defects and gossiping, this is not humility. It is instead thinking that you are the judge of others. The prophet says: "I will leave as a remnant in your midst a people humble and lowly." This is a grace, and we must ask for this grace, that the Church may be humble, that I may be humble, that each one of us may be humble.

The second trait of the People of God is being poor. Poverty is the first of the Beatitudes, but what does it mean to be poor in spirit? It means being attached only to God's treasures. It definitely does not mean a Church that exists attached to money, that thinks about money, that thinks about how to earn money. For example, someone who innocently said to the people that they had to make an offering in order to pass through the Holy Door. This is not the Church of Jesus, this is the Church of those chief priests, attached to money.

Think of the story of Deacon Lawrence—the treasurer of the diocese—who, when the emperor asked him to bring the riches of the diocese to turn them over in order to avoid being killed, Saint Lawrence returned with the poor. Thus, the poor are actually the treasure of the Church. You can even be the head of a bank, as long as your heart is poor, not attached to money, and you place yourself at the service of others. Poverty is characterized by this detachment that leads us to serve the needy.

Last, the third trait of the People of God is that they shall seek refuge in the name of the Lord. This too brings up a very direct question: Where do I place my trust? In power, in friends, in money? In the Lord!

This is the legacy that the Lord promises us: "I will leave in the midst of you a people humble and lowly. They shall seek refuge in the name of the Lord." Humble, because they feel they are sinners; poor, because their heart is attached to God's treasures, and if they have them it is only to administer them; seeking refuge in the Lord, because they know that the Lord alone can guarantee what is good for them. This is why Jesus had to tell the chief priests, "who did not understand these things," that "a harlot would enter the kingdom of God before them." Let us ask that he give us a humble heart, a heart that is poor, and above all a heart that seeks refuge in the Lord, because the Lord never disappoints.

Readings from the Fathers of the Church

Saint Ambrose,
Lawrence shows the true treasures of the Church

How wonderful it is that it is said, when the Church ransoms groups of prisoners: "They have been ransomed by Christ"! Behold the gold that is praiseworthy, behold the gold that is serviceable, behold the gold of Christ that brings freedom from death, behold the gold through which modesty is ransomed, chastity is preserved! [. . .]

Such is the gold that the holy martyr Lawrence kept for the Lord. In fact, to those who asked him about the treasures of the Church, he promised to display it. The next day he led in the poor. Asked where the promised treasures were, he pointed to the poor, saying: "These are the treasures of the Church." And they are truly treasures, who have within them Christ, who have within them the faith of Christ. [. . .]

Lawrence displayed these treasures and was victorious because not even the persecutor could take them away. [. . .] Lawrence, who had preferred to distribute the Church's gold to the poor rather than set it aside for the persecutor, obtained by the singular shrewdness of his foresight the rich crown of martyrdom. [. . .]

No one can say: "Why does the poor man live?" No one can complain because prisoners have been ransomed; no one can hurl accusations because more room has been made to bury the remains of the faithful; no one can moan because deceased Christians are resting in a tomb. In these three cases it is permissible to break, melt, sell the vessels of the Church, even if they have already been consecrated.

The New Wine of Mercy

Twenty-Seventh Sunday of Ordinary Time

☩

Matthew 21:33–43

40 "What will the owner of the vineyard do to those tenants
when he comes?" 41 They answered him, "He will put those
wretched men to a wretched death and lease his vineyard to
other tenants who will give him the produce at the proper
times."

This Sunday's liturgy offers us the parable of the tenants
to whom a landowner lends the vineyard he has planted,
and then goes away (Mt 21:33–43). This is how the loyalty of
these tenants is tested: the vineyard is entrusted to them, they
are to tend it, make it bear fruit, and deliver its harvest to the
owner. When the time comes to harvest the grapes, the land-
lord sends his servants to pick the fruit. However, the vineyard tenants assume a possessive attitude. They do not
consider themselves to be simple supervisors, but rather
landowners, and they refuse to hand over the harvest. They
mistreat the servants, to the point of killing them. The landowner is patient with them. He sends more servants, larger in

number than the previous ones, but the result is the same. In the end, he patiently decides to send his own son. But those tenants, prisoners to their own possessive behavior, also kill the son, reasoning that, in this way, they will have the inheritance.

This narrative allegorically illustrates the reproaches of the prophets in the story of Israel. It is a history that belongs to us. It is about the Covenant that God wished to establish with mankind and in which he also called us to participate. Like any other love story, this story of the Covenant has its positive moments, but it is also marked by betrayal and rejection. In order to make us understand how God the Father responds to the rejection of his love and his proposal of an alliance, the Gospel passage puts a question on the lips of the owner of the vineyard: "What will the owner of the vineyard do to those tenants when he comes?" (v. 40). This question emphasizes that God's disappointment at the wicked behavior of mankind is not the last word! This is the great novelty of Christianity: a God who, even though disappointed by our mistakes and our sins, does not fail to keep his Word, does not give up, and, most of all, does not seek vengeance!

My brothers and sisters, God does not avenge himself. God loves; he does not avenge himself. He waits for us, to forgive us, to embrace us. Through the "rejected stones"—and Christ is the first stone that the builders rejected—through situations of weakness and sin, God continues to circulate "the new wine" of his vineyard, namely mercy. This is the new wine of the Lord's vineyard: mercy. There is only one obstacle to the tenacious and tender will of God: our arrogance and our conceit, which, at times, also become violence! Faced with these attitudes where no fruit is produced, the Word of God retains all its power to reprimand and reproach: "Therefore, I say to you, the kingdom of God will be taken away from you and given to a people that will produce its fruit" (v. 43).

The urgency of replying with good fruits to the call of the Lord, who asks us to become his vineyard, helps us understand what is new and original about the Christian faith. It is not so much the sum of precepts and moral norms, but rather, it is first and foremost a proposal of love, which God makes through Jesus and continues to make with mankind. It is an invitation to enter into this love story, by becoming a lively and open vine, rich in fruits and hope for everyone. A closed vineyard can become wild and produce wild grapes. We are called to leave this vineyard to put ourselves at the service of our brothers and sisters who are not with us, in order to encourage each other, to remind ourselves that we must be the Lord's vineyard in every environment, even the more distant and challenging ones.

Dear brothers and sisters, let us invoke the intercession of the Most Holy Mary, so that she may help us to be everywhere, in particular in the peripheries of society, the vineyard that the Lord planted for the good of all and to bring the new wine of the Lord's mercy.

Readings from the Fathers of the Church

Saint Gregory the Great,
God takes care of the flock,
even when the shepherds make mistakes

Does almighty God perhaps abandon his own flock because of our negligence? Of course not. In fact, he feeds it directly, as he promised through the prophet, and he instructs those predestined to life with the prodding of misfortunes and with the spirit of compunction. [. . .]

The elect are admitted into the heavenly homeland, purified by the ministry of the priests, while these latter plunge toward the torments of hell on account of their reprehensible life. To what then shall I compare unworthy priests, if not to the water of baptism which, erasing the sins of the baptized, ushers them into the Kingdom of Heaven, but then has to be put out with the garbage? Let us fear, brothers, lest our ministry meet such a fate. Let us do all we can every day to be purified from our faults, so that these may not enchain our own life, through which almighty God purifies others from evil every day. Let us reflect without respite on what we are, let us meditate on our ministry and become aware of the responsibilities we have assumed. Let us pose to ourselves every day the questions we will have to answer before the Judge. We should also look after ourselves, so as not to neglect our neighbor, in such a way that whoever approaches us may be as it were seasoned with the salt of our word.

The Church's Breadth
Is the Kingdom of God
Twenty-Eighth Sunday of Ordinary Time

+

Matthew 22:1–14

8 "Then he said to his servants, 'The feast is ready, but those who were invited were not worthy to come. 9 Go out, therefore, into the main roads and invite to the feast whomever you find.' 10 The servants went out into the streets and gathered all they found, bad and good alike, and the hall was filled with guests. 11 But when the king came in to meet the guests he saw a man there not dressed in a wedding garment. 12 He said to him, 'My friend, how is it that you came in here without a wedding garment?' But he was reduced to silence."

I n this Sunday's Gospel (Mt 22:1–14), Jesus speaks to us about the response given to the invitation from God—who is represented by a king—to participate in a wedding banquet. The invitation has three characteristics: *freely offered, broad,* and *universal.* Many people were invited, but something surprising happened: none of the intended guests came to take part in the feast, saying they had other things to do; indeed, some were indifferent, impertinent, even annoyed. God is good to us, he freely offers us his friendship, he freely offers us his joy, his salvation. But so often we do not accept his gifts. Instead, we place our practical concerns and our interests first. And when the Lord is calling to us, it so often seems to annoy us.

Some of the intended guests went so far as to abuse and kill the servants who delivered the invitation. But despite the lack of response from those called, God's plan is never interrupted. In facing the rejection of the first invitees, he is not discouraged. He does not cancel the feast, but makes another invitation, expanding it beyond all reasonable limits, and sends his servants into the town squares and the byways to gather anyone they find. These, however, are ordinary, poor, neglected, and marginalized people, good and bad alike— even bad people are invited—without distinction. And the hall is filled with "the excluded." The Gospel, rejected by some, is unexpectedly welcomed in many other hearts.

The goodness of God has no bounds and does not discriminate against anyone. For this reason the banquet of the Lord's gifts is universal, for everyone. Everyone is given the opportunity to respond to the invitation, to his call; no one has the right to feel privileged or to claim an exclusive right. All of this induces us to break the habit of conveniently placing ourselves at the center, as did the high priests and the Pharisees. One must not do this; we must open ourselves to the peripheries, also acknowledging that, at the margins too, even one who is cast aside and scorned by society is the object of God's generosity. We are all called not to reduce the Kingdom of God to the confines of the "little church"—our "tiny little church"—but to enlarge the Church to the dimensions of the Kingdom of God. However, there is one condition: wedding attire must be worn, that is, charity toward God and neighbor must be shown.

Let us entrust the tragedies and the hopes of so many of our excluded, weak, outcast, scorned brothers and sisters, as well as of those who are persecuted for reasons of faith, to the intercession of Most Holy Mary, and let us also invoke her protection upon the work of the Synod of Bishops, who meet in the Vatican.

Readings from the Fathers of the Church

Saint Cyprian,
The Kingdom of God is Christ himself

[In the Our Father] we ask that the Kingdom of God be recreated in us, just as we ask that his name be sanctified within us. [. . .] We ask for the coming of his Kingdom, which has been promised to us by God and has been obtained with the blood and Passion of Christ, so that we may reign together with Christ the Lord after having served him here in this world. This is what he himself promises, saying: "Come, blessed of my Father, receive the kingdom that has been prepared for you from the beginning of the world" (Mt 25:34). Dearest brothers, in reality even Christ himself can be the Kingdom of God whose coming we desire every day; we want his return to be translated into reality for us soon. In fact, since he is the Resurrection, as it is in him that we rise again, so also the Kingdom of God can be understood as Christ, because it is in him that we will reign. So, it is right for us to invoke the Kingdom of God, meaning the heavenly kingdom, because there is also an earthly kingdom; but he who has renounced the world is superior both to the honors of the world and to the earthly kingdom. And therefore he who says he belongs to God or to Christ does not desire earthly kingdoms, but those of heaven.

The Fundamental Belonging
Twenty-Ninth Sunday of Ordinary Time

✝

Matthew 22:15–21

18 Knowing their malice, Jesus said, "Why are you testing me, you hypocrites? 19 Show me the coin that pays the census tax." Then they handed him the Roman coin. 20 He said to them, "Whose image is this and whose inscription?" 21 They replied, "Caesar's." At that he said to them, "Then repay to Caesar what belongs to Caesar and to God what belongs to God."

This Sunday's Gospel (Mt 22:15–21) presents to us a new face-to-face encounter between Jesus and his adversaries. The theme addressed is that of the tribute to Caesar: a "thorny" issue about whether or not it was lawful to pay taxes to the Roman emperor, to whom Palestine was subject in Jesus' time. There were various positions. Thus, the question that the Pharisees posed to him—"Is it lawful to pay the census tax to Caesar or not?" (v. 17)—was meant to ensnare the Teacher. In fact, depending on how he responded, he could have been accused of being either for or against Rome.

. But in this case too, Jesus responds calmly and takes advantage of the malicious question in order to teach an important lesson, rising above the polemics and the alliance of his adversaries. He tells the Pharisees: "Show me the coin that pays the census tax." They present him a coin, and, observing the coin, Jesus asks: "Whose image is this and whose inscription?" The Pharisees can only answer "Caesar's." Then Jesus concludes: "Then repay to Caesar what belongs to Caesar and to God what belongs to God" (cf. vv. 19–21). On the one hand, suggesting they return to the emperor what belongs to him, Jesus declares that paying tax is not an act of idolatry, but a legal obligation to the earthly authority; on the other—and it is here that Jesus presents the "thrust" of his response—recalling the primacy of God, he asks them to render to him that which is his due as the Lord of the life and history of mankind.

The reference to Caesar's image engraved on the coin says that it is right that they feel fully—with rights and duties—citizens of the state; but symbolically it makes them think about the other image, which is imprinted on every man and woman: the image of God. He is the Lord of all, and we, who were created "in his image" (Gen 1:27), belong to him first and foremost. From the question posed to him by the Pharisees, Jesus draws a more radical and vital question for each of us, a question we can ask ourselves: *To whom do I belong?* To family, to the city, to friends, to work, to politics, to the state? Yes, of course. But first and foremost, Jesus reminds us, you belong to God. This is the fundamental belonging. It is he who has given you all that you are and have. And therefore, day by day, we can and must live our life in recognition of this fundamental belonging and in heartfelt gratitude toward our Father, who creates each one of us individually, unrepeatable, but always according to the image of his beloved Son, Jesus. It is a wondrous mystery.

Christians are called to commit themselves concretely in the human and social spheres without comparing "God" and "Caesar"; comparing God and Caesar would be a fundamentalist approach. Christians are called to commit themselves concretely in earthly realities, but illuminating them with the light that comes from God. The primary entrustment to God and hope in him do not imply an escape from reality, but rather the diligent rendering to God that which belongs to him. This is why a believer looks to the future reality, that of God, so as to live earthly life to the fullest, and to meet its challenges with courage.

May the Virgin Mary help us to always live in conformity with the image of God that we bear within us, inside, also offering our contribution to the building of the earthly city.

Readings from the Fathers of the Church

Tertullian,
We are the image of God

Imagine, therefore, God [at the moment of the creation of man] entirely busy with and interested in this mud, with his hand, with his intelligence, with his activity, with his thought, with his wisdom, with his providence, and above all with that affection which dictated for him the features of the body: because whatever the form into which that mud would be shaped, that was to be the pattern for Christ, who would become man, that is mud, and was to be the pattern for the Word, who would become flesh, which was then earth. In fact, the Father had already said this to the Son: "Let us make man in our image and likeness; and God made man"—evidently the one he had molded—"in the image of God He made him" (cf. Gn 1:26–27), meaning in the image of Christ. God is in fact the Word who, being in the image of God, did not deem it robbery to be equal to God. Therefore, that mud, on which there had already been placed the image of Christ who was to come in the flesh, was not only God's work, but God's pledge.

The Face of the Father
and the Face of the Brother
Thirtieth Sunday of Ordinary Time

✝

Matthew 22:34–40

35 And one of them [a scholar of the law] tested him by asking, 36 "Teacher, which commandment in the law is the greatest?" 37 He said to him, "You shall love the Lord, your God, with all your heart, with all your soul, and with all your mind. 38 This is the greatest and the first commandment. 39 The second is like it: You shall love your neighbor as yourself. 40 The whole law and the prophets depend on these two commandments."

Today's Gospel reading (Mt 22:34–40) reminds us that the whole of Divine Law can be summed up in our love for God and neighbor. Matthew the Evangelist recounts that several Pharisees colluded to put Jesus to the test (cf. vv. 34–35). One of them, a doctor of the law, asked him this question: "Teacher, which commandment in the law is the greatest?" (v. 36). Jesus, quoting the Book of Deuteronomy, answered: "You shall love the Lord, your God, with all your heart, with all your soul and with all your mind. This is the greatest and the first commandment" (vv. 37–38). And he could have stopped there. Yet, Jesus adds something that was not asked by the doctor of the law. He says, in fact: "The second is like it: You shall love your neighbor as yourself" (v. 39). And in this case too, Jesus does not invent the second commandment, but takes it from the Book of Leviticus. The novelty is in his placing these two commandments together—love for God and love for neighbor—revealing that they are in fact inseparable and complementary, two sides of the same coin. You cannot love God without loving your neighbor and you cannot love your neighbor without loving God. Pope Benedict gave us a beautiful commentary on this topic in his first encyclical, *Deus Caritas Est* (nn. 16–18).

In effect, the visible sign a Christian can show in order to witness to his love for God to the world, to others, and to his family, is the love he bears for his brothers. The commandment to love God and neighbor is the first, not because it is at the top of the list of commandments. Jesus does not place it at the pinnacle but at the center, because it is from the heart that everything must go out and to which everything must return and refer.

In the Old Testament, the requirement to be holy, in the image of God, who is holy, included the duty to care for the most vulnerable people, such as the stranger, the orphan, and the widow (cf. Ex 22:20–23). Jesus brings this Covenant law to fulfillment; he who unites in himself, in his flesh, divinity and humanity, a single mystery of love.

Now, in the light of this Word of Jesus, love is the measure of faith, and faith is the soul of love. We can no longer separate a religious life, a pious life, from service to brothers and sisters, to the real brothers and sisters that we encounter. We can no longer separate prayer—that encounter with God in the Sacraments—from listening to our brother and listening to a closeness to his life, especially to his wounds. Remember this: love is the measure of faith. How much do you love? Each one answer silently. How is your faith? My faith is as I love. And faith is the soul of love.

In the middle of the dense forest of rules and regulations—the legalisms of past and present—Jesus makes an opening through which one can catch a glimpse of two faces: the face of the Father and the face of the brother. He does not give us two formulas or two precepts: there are no precepts or formulas. He gives us two faces, actually only one real face, that of God reflected in many faces, because in the face of each brother, especially of the smallest, the most fragile, the defenseless and needy, there is God's own image. And we must ask ourselves: When we meet one of these brothers, are we able to recognize the face of God in him? Are we able to do this?

In this way, Jesus offers to all the fundamental criteria on which to base one's life. But, above all, he gave us the Holy Spirit, who allows us to love God and neighbor as he does, with a free and generous heart.

With the intercession of Mary, our Mother, let us open ourselves to welcome this gift of love, to walk forever with this twofold law, which really has only one facet: the law of love.

Readings from the Fathers of the Church

Saint Maximus the Confessor,
Without charity all is vanity of vanities

He who loves God puts the knowledge of him before all the things that he has made, and with lively desire incessantly perseveres in it.

If all things have been made by God and for God, God is greater than the things he has made. He who leaves aside the better thing and gives himself to inferior things shows that he puts before God the things that he has made. [. . .]

He who loves God cannot help but love every man as himself, even if he abhors the passions of those who are not yet purified. And therefore, seeing their conversion and their improvement, he savors an immeasurable and inexpressible joy. [. . .]

He who glimpses in his own heart a trace of anger toward any man, whatever his error may be, is completely alienated from the love of God, because the love of God by no means tolerates hatred for man. [. . .]

He who loves God certainly loves his neighbor as well. And he does not hold on to wealth, but administers it in a way worthy of God, offering it to those who are in need.

He who gives alms in imitation of God knows no distinction between bad and good or just and unjust in the things necessary to the body, but distributes to all equally according to need, although in opting for the good he prefers the virtuous over the wicked.

Not Supermen, Simply Saints
All Saints

Matthew 5:1–12

2 He began to teach them, saying: 3 "Blessed are the poor in spirit, for theirs is the kingdom of heaven."

The Solemnity of All Saints is "our" celebration: not because we are good, but because the sanctity of God has touched our lives. The saints are not perfect models, but people *through whom God has passed*. We can compare them to the church windows, which allow light to enter in different shades of color. The saints are our brothers and sisters who have welcomed the light of God into their hearts and have passed it on to the world, each according to his or her own "hue." But they were all transparent; they fought to remove the stains and the darkness of sin, so as to enable the gentle light of God to pass through. This is life's purpose: to enable God's light to pass through. It is the purpose of our life too.

Indeed, today in the Gospel, Jesus addresses his followers,

all of us, telling us we are "Blessed" (Mt 5:3). It is the word with which he begins his sermon, which is the "Gospel," Good News, because it is the path to happiness. Those who are with Jesus are blessed; they are happy. Happiness is not in having something or in becoming someone. No. True happiness is being with the Lord and living for love. Do you believe this? True happiness is not in having something or in becoming someone; true happiness is being with the Lord and living for love. Do you believe this? We must go forth, believing in this.

The ingredients for a happy life are called *Beatitudes*: blessed are the simple, the humble, who make room for God, who are able to weep for others and for their own mistakes, who remain meek, fight for justice, are merciful to all, safeguard purity of heart, always work for peace and abide in joy, do not hate, and, even when suffering, respond to evil with good. These are the Beatitudes. They do not require conspicuous gestures. They are not for supermen, but for those who live the trials and toils of every day, for us. This is how the saints are: like everyone, they breathe air polluted by the evil there is in the world, but, on the journey, they never lose sight of *Jesus' road map,* that indicated in the Beatitudes, which is like *the map of Christian life*.

Today is the celebration of those who have reached the destination indicated by this map: not only the saints on the calendar, but many brothers and sisters "next door," whom we may have met and known. Today is a *family celebration* of many simple, hidden people who in reality help God to move

the world forward. And there are so many of them today!
There are so many of them! Thanks to these unknown brothers and sisters who help God to move the world forward, who
live among us. Let us salute them all with a nice round of ap-
plause!

First of all—the first Beatitude says—they are "poor in
spirit" (v. 3). What does this mean? That they do not live for
success, power, and money; they know that those who set
aside treasure for themselves are not rich toward God (cf. Lk
12:21). Rather, they believe that the Lord is life's treasure, and
love for neighbor is the only true source of gain. At times we
are dissatisfied due to something we lack, or worried if we are
not considered as we would like; let us remember that our
Beatitude is not here, but in the Lord and in love. Only with
him, only by loving do we live as blessed.

Last, I would like to quote another Beatitude, which is not
found in the Gospel but at the end of the Bible, and it speaks
of the end of life: "Blessed are the dead who die in the Lord"
(Rev 14:13). Tomorrow we will be called to accompany with
prayer our deceased, so they may be forever joyful in the Lord.
Let us remember our loved ones with gratitude and let us
pray for them.

**May the Mother of God, Queen of the Saints and Gate of
Heaven, intercede for our journey of holiness and for our
loved ones who have gone before us and who have already
departed for the heavenly Homeland.**

Readings from the Fathers of the Church

Saint Ignatius of Antioch,
The faith of the saints

I glorify Jesus Christ God who has made you so wise. In fact, I have confirmed that you are perfect in an unshakable faith, nailed as it were to the Cross of the Lord Jesus Christ in the flesh and in the spirit and grounded in charity, in the blood of Christ, being full of ardor for our Lord, who truly descends from the lineage of David according to the flesh (cf. Rom 1:3), Son of God according to the will and power of God, truly born of the Virgin, baptized by John, so that "all justice might be fulfilled by him" (cf. Mt 3:15). Truly under Pontius Pilate and the tetrarch Herod nailed for us in the flesh, we are the fruit of his blessed Passion for whom by his Resurrection he has raised a standard unto the ages for his holy and faithful ones, Jews and pagans, in the one body of his Church.

In fact, he suffered all these things for us that we may be saved; and he truly suffered, as he also truly rose again, not as some unbelievers say according to whom he suffered in appearance, whereas they themselves are appearances; and as they think so will it happen to them to become incorporeal and like spirits. [. . .]

To this I exhort you, dearly beloved, knowing that you also think this way.

Live Every Day
As If It Were the Last
Thirty-Second Sunday of Ordinary Time

+

Matthew 25:1–13

10 "While they went off to buy it, the bridegroom came and those who were ready went into the wedding feast with him. Then the door was locked. 11 Afterwards the other virgins came and said, 'Lord, Lord, open the door for us!' 12 But he said in reply, 'Amen, I say to you, I do not know you.' 13 Therefore, stay awake, for you know neither the day nor the hour."

This Sunday, the Gospel (Mt 25:1–13) indicates the condition that would allow us to enter the Kingdom of Heaven, and it does so with the parable of the ten virgins: it is about those maiden brides who were designated to welcome and accompany the bridegroom to the wedding ceremony and, since at that time it was customary to celebrate the ceremony at night, the maiden brides were provided with lamps. The parable states that five of these maidens are wise and five are foolish. Indeed, the wise ones have brought oil for their lamps, while the foolish have brought none. The bridegroom's arrival is delayed, and they all fall asleep. At midnight the bridegroom's arrival is announced. At that moment, the foolish maidens realize they have no oil for their lamps, and they ask the wise ones for some. But the latter reply that they cannot give them any because there would not be enough for everyone. Thus, while the foolish maidens go in search of oil, the bridegroom arrives; the wise maidens go in with him to the marriage feast, and the door is shut. The five foolish maidens return too late; they knock on the door, but the response is "I do not know you" (v. 12), and they remain outside.

What does Jesus wish to teach us with this parable? He reminds us that we must be ready for the encounter with him. Many times, in the Gospel, Jesus exhorts keeping watch, and he also does so at the end of this narrative. He says: "Therefore, stay awake, for you know neither the day nor the hour" (v. 13). But with this parable he tells us that keeping watch means not only not to sleep, but to be ready. In fact, all the maidens are asleep before the bridegroom's arrival, but upon waking some are ready and others are not. Thus, here is the meaning of being wise and prudent: *it is a matter of not waiting until the last minute of our lives to cooperate with the grace of God, but rather to do so now*. It would be good to consider for a moment: one day will be the last. If it were today, how prepared am I? But I must do this and that. . . . Be ready as if it were the last day. This does us good!

The lamp is a symbol of the faith that illuminates our life, while the oil is a symbol of the charity that nourishes the light of faith, making it fruitful and credible. The condition for being prepared for the encounter with the Lord is not only faith, but a Christian life abundant with love and charity for our neighbor. If we allow ourselves to be guided by what seems more comfortable, by seeking our own interests, then our life becomes barren, incapable of giving life to others, and we accumulate no reserve of oil for the lamp of our faith. And this—faith—will be extinguished at the moment of the Lord's coming, or even before. If instead we are watchful and seek to do good, with acts of love, of sharing, of service to a neighbor in difficulty, then we can be at peace while we wait for the bridegroom to come. The Lord can come at any moment, and even the slumber of death does not frighten us, because we have a reserve of oil, accumulated through everyday good works. Faith inspires charity and charity safeguards faith.

May the Virgin Mary help our faith to be ever more effective through charity, so that our lamp may already shine here on the earthly journey, and then forever, at the marriage feast in heaven.

Readings from the Fathers of the Church

Saint Ephrem the Syrian, Keep watch in body and soul

Jesus said: "No one knows that hour, not even the angels, nor even the Son of man" (cf. Mt 24:36), so that the disciples would not ask him about the time of his coming. "It is not for you to know the times and the moments" (Acts 1:7).

He has kept it hidden from us so that we would continue to keep watch, and each of us should think that this coming could happen during the course of his life. If in fact the time of his coming had been revealed, his first coming would have been in vain, nor would the peoples and the ages have desired that he should come. He has nevertheless said that he will come, but he has not specified when. And thus all eras and generations are thirsty for him. [. . .]

Keep watch, because when the body goes to sleep, nature gets the upper hand and our activities are not directed by our will, but by the impulse of nature. When the heavy torpor of weakness and sadness dominates the soul, the enemy has the upper hand over it and leads it against its own desires. [. . .] For this reason, the Lord calls us to vigilance over soul and body, to keep the body from sinking into a heavy sleep and the soul into a lethargy generated by indolence.

Make the Gifts of God Bear Fruit

Thirty-Third Sunday of Ordinary Time

✝

Matthew 25:14–30

23 "His master said to him, 'Well done, my good and faithful servant. Since you were faithful in small matters, I will give you great responsibilities. Come, share your master's joy.' 24 Then the one who had received the one talent came forward and said, 'Master, I knew you were a demanding person, harvesting where you did not plant and gathering where you did not scatter; 25 so out of fear I went off and buried your talent in the ground. Here it is back.' 26 His master said to him in reply, 'You wicked, lazy servant! So you knew that I harvest where I did not plant and gather where I did not scatter? 27 Should you not then have put my money in the bank so that I could have got it back with interest on my return? 28 Now then! Take the talent from him and give it to the one with ten. 29 For to everyone who has, more will be given and he will grow rich; but from the one who has not, even what he has will be taken away.' "

The Gospel this Sunday is the parable of the talents. The passage from Saint Matthew (25:14–30) tells of a man who, before setting off on a journey, calls his servants and entrusts his assets to them in talents, which are extremely valuable ancient coins. That master entrusts five talents to the first servant, two to the second, and one to the third. During the master's absence, the three servants must earn a profit from this patrimony. The first and second servants each double the initial value of the capital. The third, however, for fear of losing it all, buries the talent he received in a hole. Upon the master's return, the first two receive praise and rewards, while the third, who returned only the coin he had received, is reproached and punished.

The meaning of this is clear. The man in the parable represents Jesus, we are the servants, and the talents are the inheritance that the Lord entrusts to us. What is the inheritance? His Word, the Eucharist, faith in the Heavenly Father, his forgiveness . . . In other words, so many things, his most precious treasures. This is the inheritance that he entrusts to us, not only to safeguard, but to make fruitful! While in common usage the term "talent" indicates a pronounced individual quality—for example, talent in music, in sport, and so on—in the parable, talent represent the riches of the Lord, which he entrusts to us so that we make them bear fruit. The hole dug into the soil by the "wicked, lazy servant" (v. 26) points to the fear of risk, which blocks creativity and the fruitfulness of love, because the fear of the risks of love stop us.

Jesus does not ask us to store his grace in a safe! Jesus does not ask us for this. Instead, he wants us to use it to benefit others. All the goods that we have received are to give to others, and thus they increase, as if he were to tell us: "Here is my mercy, my tenderness, my forgiveness: take them and make ample use of them." And what have we done with them? Whom have we "infected" with our faith? How many people have we encouraged with our hope? How much love have we shared with our neighbor? These are questions that will do us good to ask ourselves. Any environment, even the farthest and most impractical, can become a place where our talents can bear fruit. There are no situations or places precluded from the Christian presence and witness. The witness which Jesus asks of us is not closed, but is open; it is in our hands.

This parable urges us not to conceal our faith and our belonging to Christ, not to bury the Word of the Gospel, but to let it circulate in our lives, in our relationships, in concrete situations, as a strength which galvanizes, which purifies, which renews. Similarly, forgiveness, which the Lord grants us particularly in the Sacrament of Reconciliation, should not be hidden: let us not keep it closed within ourselves, but let us allow it to emit its power, which brings down the walls that our egoism has raised, which enables us to take the first step in strained relationships, to resume the dialogue where there is no longer communication. . . . And so forth. Allow these talents, these gifts, these presents that the Lord has given us to be, to grow, to bear fruit for others, with our witness.

I think it would be a fine gesture for each of you to pick up the Gospel at home today, the Gospel of Saint Matthew, chapter 25, verses 14 to 30, and read this, and then meditate a bit on what it is saying: "These talents, these treasures, all that God has given me, all things spiritual, all goodness, the

Word of God, how do I make these grow in others? Or do I merely store them in a safe?"

Moreover, the Lord does not give the same things to everyone in the same way. He knows us personally and entrusts us with what is right for us. But in everyone, in all, there is something equal: the same, immense trust. God trusts us. God has hope in us! And this is the same for everyone. Let us not disappoint him! Let us not be misled by fear, but let us reciprocate trust with trust!

The Virgin Mary embodied this attitude in the fullest and most beautiful way. She received and welcomed the most sublime gift, Jesus himself, and in turn she offered him to mankind with a generous heart. Let us ask her to help us to be "good and faithful servants" in order to participate "in the joy of our Lord."

Readings from the Fathers of the Church

Saint Ambrose,
The talents to be invested

You who hear or read these things, you are everything to us: you are the interest of the one who lends, in words, not in money; you are the harvest of the farmer; you are the gold, the silver, and the precious stones of the builder. [. . .]

In your progress the Lord's gold shines, the silver is multiplied, if you preserve the divine words within you. Because "the words of the Lord are pure, they are silver tried with fire, tested by the crucible, purified seven times" (Ps 12:7). You, therefore, will make the lender rich, the farmer fruitful, you put to the test the expert "architect" (1 Cor 3:10). I do not speak with arrogance, because these merits are not so much mine as yours, merits that I hope you have.[. . .]

These are the five talents that the Lord orders be given out at interest in the spiritual sense; these are "the two bronze coins" (cf. Lk 10:35) of the New and Old Testament, which "the Samaritan" in the Gospel left behind to take care of the wounds of the man who had been stripped by the robbers.

We Will Be Judged on Love

Our Lord Jesus Christ, King of the Universe
Last Sunday of the Liturgical Year

✝

Matthew 25:31–46

37 "Then the righteous will answer him and say, 'Lord, when did we see you hungry and feed you, or thirsty and give you drink? 38 When did we see you a stranger and welcome you, or naked and clothe you? 39 When did we see you ill or in prison, and visit you?' 40 And the king will say to them in reply, 'Amen, I say to you, whatever you did for one of these least brothers of mine, you did for me.' "

On this last Sunday of the liturgical year we are celebrating the Solemnity of Christ, King of the Universe. His is a kingship of guidance, of service, and also a kingship that at the end of time will be fulfilled as judgment. Today, we have Christ before us as King, Shepherd, and Judge, who reveals the criteria for belonging to the Kingdom of God. Here are the criteria: The Gospel passage opens with a grandiose vision. Jesus, addressing his disciples, says: "When the Son of Man comes in his glory, and all the angels with him, he will sit upon his glorious throne" (Mt 25:31). It is a solemn introduction to the narrative of the Last Judgment. After having lived his earthly existence in humility and poverty, Jesus now shows himself in the divine glory that pertains to him, surrounded by hosts of angels. All of humanity is summoned before him and he exercises his authority, separating one from another, as the shepherd separates the sheep from the goats.

To those whom he has placed at his right he says: "Come, you who are blessed by my Father. Inherit the kingdom prepared for you from the foundation of the world. For I was hungry and you gave me food, I was thirsty and you gave me drink, a stranger and you welcomed me, naked and you clothed me, ill and you cared for me, in prison and you visited me" (vv. 34–36). The righteous are taken aback, because they do not recall ever having met Jesus, much less having helped him in that way, but he declares: "Whatever you did for one of these least brothers of mine, you did for me" (v. 40).

These words never cease to move us, because they reveal the extent to which God's love goes: up to the point of taking flesh, but not when we are well, when we are healthy and happy. No. But when we are in need. And in this hidden way he allows himself to be encountered; he reaches out his hand to us as a mendicant. In this way, Jesus reveals the decisive criterion of his judgment, namely, concrete love for a neighbor in difficulty. And in this way, the power of love, the Kingship of God is revealed: in solidarity with those who suffer in order to engender everywhere compassion and works of mercy.

The Parable of the Judgment continues, presenting the king who shuns those who, during their lives, did not concern themselves with the needs of their brethren. Those in this case too are surprised and ask: "Lord, when did we see you hungry or thirsty or a stranger or naked or ill or in prison, and not minister to your needs?" (v. 44). Implying: "Had we seen you, surely we would have helped you!" But the king will respond: "What you did not do for one of these least ones, you did not do for me" (v. 45). At the end of our life we will be judged on love, that is, on our concrete commitment to love and serve Jesus in our littlest and neediest brothers and sisters. That mendicant, that needy person who reaches out his hand, is Jesus; that sick person whom I must visit is Jesus; that inmate is Jesus; that hungry person is Jesus. Let us consider this. Jesus will come at the end of time to judge all nations, but he comes to us each day, in many ways, and asks us to welcome him.

> May the Virgin Mary help us to encounter him and receive him in his Word and in the Eucharist, and at the same time in brothers and sisters who suffer from hunger, disease, oppression, and injustice. May our hearts welcome him in the present of our life, so that we may be welcomed by him into the eternity of his Kingdom of light and peace.

Readings from the Fathers of the Church

Saint Caesarius of Arles, Mercy divine and human

O man, with what shamelessness do you want to ask for what you forget to give? He who in fact desires to receive mercy in heaven must grant it on this earth. And since, dearest brothers, all of us desire to receive mercy, let us live in such a way that it be our protector in this present time, just as in that future it will be the one to set us free.

There is a mercy in heaven at which one arrives through earthly works of mercy. In fact, the Scripture says: "Lord, your mercy is in heaven" (Ps 36:6). There is an earthly mercy and a heavenly, human and divine mercy. What is human mercy? Above all, paying attention to the miseries of the poor. Then what is the divine? That which grants forgiveness to sinners.

Everything that human mercy bestows on the journey of life, divine mercy will repay in the heavenly homeland. In this world, in fact, God is cold and thirsty in every poor person, as he himself says: "Whatever you did for one of these least brothers of mine, you did for me" (Mt 25:40).

The God who deigns to bestow from heaven wants to receive on earth.

Dates of the Liturgical Calendar

(Year A)

First Advent Sunday (page 3)
November 27, 2022
November 30, 2025
December 3, 2028

Immaculate Conception of the Blessed Virgin Mary
(page 7)
December 8, 2022, 2023, 2024

Third Sunday of Advent (page 11)
December 11, 2022
December 14, 2025
December 17, 2028

Fourth Sunday of Advent (page 15)
December 18, 2022
December 21, 2025
December 24, 2028

Christmas of Our Lord *(page 19)*
December 25, 2022
December 25, 2025
December 25, 2028

Feast of St. Stephen, Protomartyr *(page 23)*
December 26, 2023, 2024
December 26, 2025, 2026
December 26, 2027

Sacred Family *(page 27)*
December 30, 2022
December 28, 2025
December 31, 2028

Second Sunday of Christmastime *(page 32)*
January 1, 2023
January 4, 2026
January 7, 2029

Epiphany of Our Lord *(page 36)*
January 6, 2023
January 6, 2026
January 6, 2029

Baptism of Our Lord *(page 41)*
January 9, 2023
January 11, 2026
January 7, 2029

Second Sunday of Ordinary Time (page 45)
January 15, 2023
January 18, 2026
January 14, 2029

Third Sunday of Ordinary Time (page 49)
January 22, 2023
January 25, 2026
January 21, 2029

Feast of the Presentation of the Lord (page 54)
February 2, 2024, 2025
February 2, 2026, 2027
February 2, 2028

Fifth Sunday of Ordinary Time (page 59)
February 5, 2023
February 8, 2026
February 4, 2029

Sixth Sunday of Ordinary Time (page 63)
February 12, 2023
February 15, 2026
February 11, 2029

Seventh Sunday of Ordinary Time (page 68)
February 19, 2023
February 16, 2026
February 18, 2029

Ash Wednesday (page 72)
March 2, 2022
February 22, 2023
February 14, 2024

First Sunday of Lent (page 76)
February 26, 2023
February 22, 2026
February 18, 2029

Second Sunday of Lent (page 80)
March 5, 2023
March 1, 2026
February 25, 2029

Third Sunday of Lent (page 85)
March 12, 2023
March 8, 2026
March 4, 2029

Fourth Sunday of Lent (page 90)
March 19, 2023
March 15, 2026
March 11, 2029

Fifth Sunday of Lent (page 95)
March 26, 2023
March 22, 2026
March 18, 2029

Palm Sunday (page 99)
April 2, 2023
March 29, 2026
March 25, 2029

Holy Thursday (page 104)
April 6, 2023
April 2, 2026
March 29, 2029

Good Friday (page 108)
April 7, 2023
April 3, 2026
March 31, 2029

Easter of Resurrection (page 113)
April 9, 2023
April 5, 2026
April 1, 2029

Easter Monday (page 117)
April 10, 2023
April 6, 2026
April 2, 2029

Second Sunday of Easter (page 121)
April 16, 2023
April 12, 2026
April 8, 2029

Third Sunday of Easter (page 125)
April 23, 2023
April 19, 2026
April 15, 2029

Fourth Sunday of Easter (page 129)
April 30, 2023
April 26, 2026
April 22, 2029

Fifth Sunday of Easter (page 133)
May 7, 2023
May 3, 2026
April 29, 2029

Sixth Sunday of Easter (page 138)
May 14, 2023
May 10, 2026
May 6, 2029

Ascension of the Lord (page 142)
May 18, 2023
May 14, 2026
May 10, 2029

Pentecost (page 146)
May 28, 2023
May 24, 2026
May 20, 2029

Holy Trinity (page 150)
June 4, 2023
May 31, 2026
May 27, 2029

Eleventh Week of Ordinary Time (*page 154*)
June 18, 2023
June 14, 2026
June 17, 2029

Twelfth Sunday of Ordinary Time (*page 158*)
June 25, 2023
June 21, 2026
June 24, 2029

Thirteenth Sunday of Ordinary Time (*page 162*)
July 2, 2023
June 28, 2026
July 1, 2029

Fourteenth Sunday of Ordinary Time (*page 166*)
July 9, 2023
July 5, 2026
July 8, 2029

Fifteenth Sunday of Ordinary Time (*page 170*)
July 16, 2023
July 12, 2026
July 15, 2029

Sixteenth Sunday of Ordinary Time (*page 174*)
July 23, 2023
July 19, 2026
July 22, 2029

Seventeenth Sunday of Ordinary Time (page 178)
July 30, 2023
July 26, 2023
July 29, 2029

Eighteenth Sunday of Ordinary Time (page 182)
August 6, 2023
August 2, 2026
August 5, 2029

Nineteenth Sunday of Ordinary Time (page 187)
August 13, 2023
August 9, 2026
August 12, 2029

Assumption of the Blessed Virgin Mary (page 192)
August 15, 2024, 2025
August 15, 2026
August 15, 2029

Twentieth Sunday of Ordinary Time (page 196)
August 20, 2023
August 16, 2026
August 19, 2029

Twenty-First Sunday of Ordinary Time (page 200)
August 27, 2023
August 23, 2026
August 26, 2029

Twenty-Second Sunday of Ordinary Time (page 204)
September 3, 2023
August 30, 2026
September 2, 2029

Twenty-Third Sunday of Ordinary Time (page 208)
September 10, 2023
September 6, 2026
September 9, 2029

Twenty-Fourth Sunday of Ordinary Time (page 213)
September 17, 2023
September 13, 2026
September 16, 2029

Twenty-Fifth Sunday of Ordinary Time (page 217)
September 24, 2023
September 20, 2026
September 23, 2029

Twenty-Sixth Sunday of Ordinary Time (page 221)
October 1, 2023
September 27, 2026
September 30, 2029

Twenty-Seventh Sunday of Ordinary Time (page 226)
October 8, 2023
October 4, 2026
October 7, 2029

Twenty-Eighth Sunday of Ordinary Time (page 230)
October 15, 2023
October 11, 2026
October 14, 2029

Twenty-Ninth Sunday of Ordinary Time (page 234)
October 22, 2023
October 18, 2026
October 21, 2029

Thirtieth Sunday of Ordinary Time (page 238)
October 29, 2023
October 25, 2026
October 28, 2029

All Saints Day (page 242)
November 1, 2023
November 1, 2026
November 1, 2029

Thirty-Second Sunday of Ordinary Time (page 246)
November 12, 2023
November 8, 2026
November 11, 2029

Thirty-Third Sunday of Ordinary Time (page 250)
November 19, 2023
November 15, 2026
November 18, 2029

Our Lord Jesus Christ, King of the Universe:
Last Sunday of the Liturgical Year (page 255)
November 26, 2023
November 22, 2026
November 25, 2029

Sources

Introduction
Catechesis of Pope Francis on the Holy Mass—*Introduction*,
November 8, 2017; *General audience,* February 7, 2018.

First Advent Sunday: A New Horizon
Angelus of November 27, 2016.

Reading
Augustine, Commentary on Psalm 95, 14–15.

Immaculate Conception of the Blessed Virgin Mary: A Big "Yes"
Angelus of December 8, 2016.

Reading
Augustine, Sermon 72A, 7–8.

Third Sunday of Advent: True Joy
Angelus of September 7, 2016; Angelus of December 11, 2016.

Reading
Jerome, Commentary on Ecclesiastes, 5, 19.

Fourth Sunday of Advent: God Near to Us
Angelus of December 18, 2016; Angelus of March 20, 2017.

Reading
Augustine, Sermon 21, 2.

Christmas of Our Lord:
Feel the Father's Love with Your Hand

Angelus of January 3, 2016.

Reading
Andrew of Crete, Oration 9.

Feast of St. Stephen, Protomartyr:
Martyrs, the Ones Who Witness the Light of Truth

Angelus of December 26, 2016.

Reading
Caesarius of Arles, Sermon 225, 1–2.

Sacred Family: Communities of Love
and Reconciliation

Angelus of December 29, 2013.

Reading
Ambrose, Commentary on Luke, 8, 74–75.

Second Sunday of Christmastime:
His Closeness Never Fades

Angelus of January 5, 2014.

Reading
Pseudo-Hippolytus, Refutation of All Heresies, book X, ch. 29.

Epiphany of Our Lord: Follow the Gentle Light

Angelus of January 6, 2017.

Reading
Origen, *Selected Works,* ed. A. Colonna (Turin: Utet, 1971), pp. 109–111.

Baptism of Our Lord: The Attraction of Mildness and Humility

Angelus of January 8, 2017.

Reading

Ambrose, Meditation on Psalm 43, 78.

Second Sunday of Ordinary Time: Behold, the Lamb of God!

Angelus of January 15, 2017.

Reading

Origen, Homilies on Numbers, 22, 1.

Third Sunday of Ordinary Time: A Conversation That Changes Hearts

Angelus of January 22, 2017.

Reading

Leo the Great, Sermon 95, 1.

Feast of the Presentation of the Lord: Hope in God Never Disappoints

Homily of February 2, 2017.

Reading

Sophronius, Oration 5, 7.

Fifth Sunday of Ordinary Time: Faith Gives "Flavor" to Life

Homily of June 7, 2016; Angelus of February 5, 2017.

Reading

Chromatius of Aquileia, Commentary on Matthew, 18.

Sixth Sunday of Ordinary Time: Being Christians Not "of Façade," but of Substance

Angelus of February 12, 2017.

Reading

Dorotheus, Spiritual Teachings, 7, 79–80.

Seventh Sunday of Ordinary Time: A Christian "Revolution"

Homily of June 14, 2016; Angelus of February 19, 2017.

Reading

Ambrose, Commentary on Luke, 5, 75–79.

Ash Wednesday: Free Yourself from the Power of Appearance

Homily of June 19, 2013; Homily of March 5, 2014.

Reading

Barnabas, Epistle, ch. 19.

First Sunday of Lent: Answer Only with the Word of God

Angelus of March 5, 2017.

Reading

Augustine, Sermon 276, 1–2.

Second Sunday of Lent: The Cross, the Door of the Resurrection

Angelus of March 18, 2014; Angelus of March 12, 2017.

Reading

Justin, First Apology, 13, 55.

Third Sunday of Lent: The Thirsty Soul Before Jesus

Angelus of March 23, 2014; Angelus of March 19, 2017.

Reading

Ambrose, On the Holy Spirit, book I, 174–175, 184.

Fourth Sunday of Lent: The Road from Blindness to Light

Angelus of March 30, 2014; Angelus of March 26, 2017.

Reading

Augustine, Tractate 44 on the Gospel of John, 16–17.

Fifth Sunday of Lent: We Leave the Grave of Our Sins

Angelus of April 6, 2014.

Reading

Ambrose, Concerning Repentance, book II, ch. 7, 63, 65–68; 66, 71.

Palm Sunday: Who Am I Before the Cross of Jesus?

Homily of April 13, 2014; Homily of April 9, 2017.

Reading

Caesarius of Arles, Sermon 159, 1, 5.

Holy Thursday: A Love Without Measure

Homily of May 10, 2013; Homily of May 3, 2015; Homily of May 18, 2017.

Reading

Ignatius of Antioch, Epistle to the Ephesians, 2, 5.

Good Friday: I Will Not Leave You Orphaned;
I Give You a Mother

Homily of September 15, 2015; Homily of September 15, 2017.

Reading

Isaac of Stella, Sermon 51, 7–9, 24.

Easter of Resurrection: Stop, the Lord Is Risen!

Homily of April 16, 2017.

Reading

Augustine, Tractate 32 on the Gospel of John, 9.

Easter Monday: The Sepulchre Is Not the Last Word!

Regina Coeli of April 17, 2017.

Reading

Melito of Sardus, Easter Homily, 99–101, 103, 105.

Second Sunday of Easter: Mercy Is a
True Form of Awareness

Regina Coeli of April 23, 2017.

Reading

Ambrose, On the Mysteries, ch. 7, 34–35, 37, 42.

Third Sunday of Easter: The Word of God,
the Eucharist: They Fill Us with Joy

Regina Coeli of May 4, 2014.

Reading

Justin, First Apology, 66, 67.

Fourth Sunday of Easter: The Road from Blindness to Light

Regina Coeli of May 11, 2014.

Reading

Caesarius of Arles, Sermon 4, 4.

Fifth Sunday of Easter: The Journey of Hope

Homily of April 22, 2016; Homily of May 3, 2016.

Reading

Epistle to Diognetus, 5–6.

Sixth Sunday of Easter: Learn the Art of Loving

Regina Coeli of May 21, 2017.

Reading

Irenaeus of Lyon, Against Heresies, book III, ch. 17, 2–3.

Ascension of the Lord: The Task of the Church

Regina Coeli of May 28, 2017.

Reading

Leo the Great, Sermon 63, 3, 6.

Pentecost: With the Freedom of the Holy Spirit

Regina Coeli of June 8, 2014.

Reading

Tertullian, Prescription against Heretics, 20, 22.

Holy Trinity: The Love That Is God

Angelus of June 15, 2014; Angelus of June 11, 2017.

Reading

Augustine, Homily 7 on 1 John, 9–10.

Eleventh Week of Ordinary Time: A Gift Without Measure

Angelus of June 22, 2014.

Reading

Cyprian, On the Lord's Prayer, 18–20.

Twelfth Sunday of Ordinary Time: The Mission Is Not Under the Banner of Tranquillity

Angelus of June 25, 2017.

Reading

Tertullian, Apology, ch. 50.

Thirteenth Sunday of Ordinary Time: A Transparent Heart

Angelus of July 2, 2017.

Reading

Augustine, Commentary on Galatians, 38.

Fourteenth Sunday of Ordinary Time: Jesus Does Not Take Away Our Cross, but Carries It with Us

Angelus of July 9, 2017.

Reading

Ambrose, Meditation on Isaac, 10.

Fifteenth Sunday of Ordinary Time: Reclamation of Our Heart

Angelus of July 16, 2017.

Reading

Evagrius Ponticus, On Prayer, 35–44.

Sixteenth Sunday of Ordinary Time:
Imitate God's Patience

Angelus of July 20, 2014; Angelus of July 23, 2017.

Reading

Tertullian, On Prayer, ch. 29.

Seventeenth Sunday of Ordinary Time:
The Treasure That Is Jesus

Angelus of July 27, 2014.

Reading

John Chrysostom, In Praise of Paul, 2, 4.

Eighteenth Sunday of Ordinary Time:
Compassionate Eucharist

Angelus of August 3, 2014.

Reading

John Chrysostom, Homilies on Matthew, 50, 3.

Nineteenth Sunday of Ordinary Time:
In the Church Boat

Angelus of August 13, 2017.

Reading

Ambrose, Commentary on Luke, 4, 70–71.

Assumption of the Blessed Virgin Mary:
The Power of Humility

Angelus of August 15, 2017.

Reading

Ambrose, Commentary on Luke, 2, 14–17.

Twentieth Sunday of Ordinary Time:
The Courage of Prayer

Angelus of August 20, 2017.

Reading

Basil the Great, On the Holy Spirit, ch. 15, 35–36.

Twenty-First Sunday of Ordinary Time:
A Heart as Firm as Stone

Angelus of August 24, 2014; Angelus of August 27, 2017.

Reading

Ambrose, Commentary on Luke, ch. 6, 97–98.

Twenty-Second Sunday of Ordinary Time:
There Is No True Love Without Sacrifice

Angelus of September 3, 2017.

Reading

Augustine, City of God, book X, ch. 6.

Twenty-Third Sunday of Ordinary Time:
Brotherly Correction

Angelus of September 7, 2014.

Reading

Augustine, Homily 7 on 1 John, 11.

Twenty-Fourth Sunday of Ordinary Time:
A Mercy Without Limits

Angelus of September 17, 2017.

Reading

Polycarp, Epistle to the Philippians, ch. 6.

Twenty-Fifth Sunday of Ordinary Time:
God Does Not Exclude Anyone

Angelus of September 24, 2017.

Reading

Gregory the Great, Pastoral Rule, book I, ch. 5.

Twenty-Sixth Sunday of Ordinary Time:
A Poor, Humble Church That Trusts in the Lord

Homily of December 15, 2015; Homily of December 13, 2016.

Reading

Ambrose, On the Duties of the Clergy, book II, ch. 28, 138–142.

Twenty-Seventh Sunday of Ordinary Time:
The New Wine of Mercy

Angelus of October 8, 2017.

Reading

Gregory the Great, Homilies on the Gospels, 1, 17, 18.

Twenty-Eighth Sunday of Ordinary Time:
The Church's Breadth Is the Kingdom of God

Angelus of October 12, 2014.

Reading

Cyprian, On the Lord's Prayer, 13–14.

Twenty-Ninth Sunday of Ordinary Time:
The Fundamental Belonging

Angelus of October 22, 2017.

Reading

Tertullian, On the Resurrection of the Flesh, ch. 6.

Thirtieth Sunday of Ordinary Time:
The Face of the Father and the Face of the Brother
Angelus of October 26, 2014.

Reading
Maximus the Confessor, On Charity, ch. 1, 4–5, 13, 15, 23–24.

All Saints Day: Not Supermen, Simply Saints
Angelus of November 1, 2017.

Reading
Ignatius of Antioch, Epistle to the Smyrnaeans, 1–2, 4.

Thirty-Second Sunday of Ordinary Time:
Live Every Day As If It Were the Last
Angelus of November 12, 2017.

Reading
Ephrem the Syrian, Commentary on Tatian's Diatessaron, ch. 18, 15, 17.

Thirty-Third Sunday of Ordinary Time:
Make the Gifts of God Bear Fruit
Angelus of November 16, 2014.

Reading
Ambrose, On Faith, book V, prologue 9–10.

Our Lord Jesus Christ, King of the Universe:
Last Sunday of the Liturgical Year:
We Will Be Judged on Love
Angelus of November 26, 2017.

Reading
Caesarius of Arles, Sermon 25, 1.